ON THE
OF THE SPACE
PIRATES

A TOM CORBETT Space Cadet Adventure

CAREY ROCKWELL

WILLY LEY *Technical Adviser*

1st WORLD
LIBRARY
Literary Society

On the Trail of the Space Pirates

Carey Rockwell

© 1st World Library, 2007
PO Box 2211
Fairfield, IA 52556
www.1stworldlibrary.com
First Edition

LCCN: 2007930753

Softcover ISBN: 978-1-4218-4801-3
Hardcover ISBN: 978-1-4218-4704-7
eBook ISBN: 978-1-4218-4898-3

Purchase *"On the Trail of the Space Pirates"*
as a traditional bound book at:
www.1stWorldLibrary.com/purchase.asp?ISBN=978-1-4218-4801-3

1st World Library is a literary, educational organization
dedicated to:

- Creating a free internet library of downloadable ebooks

- Hosting writing competitions and offering book publishing
scholarships.

Interested in more 1st World Library books? contact:
literacy@1stworldlibrary.com
Check us out at: www.1stworldlibrary.com

1ˢᵗ World Library Literary Society

Giving Back to the World

"If you want to work on the core problem, it's early school literacy."

- James Barksdale, former CEO of Netscape

"No skill is more crucial to the future of a child, or to a democratic and prosperous society, than literacy."

- Los Angeles Times

"Literacy... means far more than learning how to read and write... The aim is to transmit... knowledge and promote social participation."

- UNESCO

"Literacy is not a luxury, it is a right and a responsibility. If our world is to meet the challenges of the twenty-first century we must harness the energy and creativity of all our citizens."

- President Bill Clinton

"Parents should be encouraged to read to their children, and teachers should be equipped with all available techniques for teaching literacy, so the varying needs and capacities of individual kids can be taken into account."

- Hugh Mackay

CHAPTER 1

"ALL ABOARD!"

A metallic voice rasped over the loud-speakers and echoed through the lofty marble and aluminum concourse of the New Chicago Monorail Terminal. "Atom City express on Track Seven! Space Academy first stop! Passengers for Space Academy will please take seats in the first six cars!"

As the crowd of people waiting in the concourse surged through the gate leading to Track Seven, three boys in the royal-blue uniforms of the Space Cadet Corps slowly picked up their plastic space bags and joined the mass of travelers.

Wearily, they drifted with the crowd and stepped on the slidestairs leading down to the monorail platform. In the lead, Tom Corbett, the command cadet of the unit, a tall, curly-haired boy of eighteen, slouched against the handrail and looked back at his two unit-mates, Roger Manning and Astro. Manning, a slender cadet, with close-cropped blond hair, was yawning and blinking his eyes sleepily, while Astro, the third member of the unit, a head taller than either of his unit-mates and fifty pounds heavier, stood flat-footed on the step, eyes closed, his giant bulk swaying slightly with the motion of the slidestairs.

"Huh! A real snappy unit!" Tom muttered to himself.

"Hmmm? What?" Roger blinked and stared bleary-eyed at Tom.

"Nothing, Roger," Tom replied. "I only hope you guys can stay awake long enough to get on the monorail."

"It's your own fault, Tom," rumbled Astro in his bull-like voice. "If your family hadn't thrown so many parties for us while we were on leave, we'd have had more sleep."

"I didn't hear any complaints then," snorted Tom. "Just get into the car before you cork off, will you? I'm in no shape to carry you."

Seconds later, the slidestairs deposited the three boys on the platform and they slowly made their way through the crowd toward the forward cars of the monorail. Entering the third car, they found three seats together and collapsed into their luxurious softness.

"Oh, brother!" Tom groaned as he curled himself into the cushions, "I'm going to sleep all the way to the Academy."

"I'm asleep already," mumbled Roger, his voice muffled by his cap pulled low over his face.

Suddenly Astro sat bolt upright. "I'm hungry!" he announced.

"Oh, no!" moaned Tom.

"Why, you overgrown Venusian ape, Mrs. Corbett gave you dinner less than an hour ago!" Roger complained. "Steak, French fries, beans, corn, pie, ice cream...."

"Two helpings," chimed in Tom.

"And now you're hungry!" Roger was incredulous.

"Can't help it," calmly answered Astro. "I'm a big guy, that's all." He began digging through his space bag for an apple Mrs. Corbett had thoughtfully provided.

Tom finally stirred and sat up. He had learned a long time ago the futility of trying to deny Astro's Gargantuan appetite. "There's a dining car on this section of the monorail, Astro," he said, slapping a crumpled mass of credits into the Venusian's hamlike hand. "Here. Have yourself a good time." He slumped back in his seat and closed his eyes.

"Yeah," growled Roger, "and when you come back, don't make any noise!"

Astro smiled. He got up carefully and climbed over his two sleeping mates. Standing in the aisle, he counted the credits Tom had given him and turned to the front of the car. Suddenly a heavy voice growled behind him.

"One side, spaceboy!"

A hand grabbed him by the shoulder and pushed him to one side. Caught off balance, Astro fell back on his sleeping unit-mates.

"Hey! What th—" stuttered Astro as he sprawled on top of his friends. The two sleepy cadets came up howling.

"Astro! What in blazes do you think you're doing?" roared Tom.

"Why, you space-brained idiot," yelled Roger, "I ought to lay one on your chin!"

There was a tangle of arms and legs and finally the three cadets struggled to their feet. Astro turned to see who had pushed him.

Two men standing at the end of the car grinned back at him.

"It was those two guys at the end of the car," explained Astro. "They pushed me!" He lumbered toward them, followed by Tom and Roger.

Stopping squarely in front of them, he demanded, "What's the big idea?"

"Go back to your beauty rest, spaceboy!" jeered the heavier of the two men and turned to his companion, adding with a snarl, "How do you like his nerve? We not only have to pay taxes to support these lazy kids and teach them how to be spacemen, but they're loud-mouthed and sassy on top of it!"

The other man, smaller and rat-faced, laughed. "Yeah, we oughta report them to their little soldier bosses at Space Academy."

Astro suddenly balled his fists and stepped forward, but Tom grabbed his arm and pulled him back while Roger eased himself between his mates and the two grinning men.

"You know, Tom," he drawled, looking the heavier of the two right in the eye, "the only thing I don't like about being a Space Cadet is having to be polite to *all* the people, including the space crawlers!"

"Why, you little punk," sneered the bigger man, "I oughta wipe up the deck with you!"

Roger smiled thinly. "Don't try it, mister. You wouldn't know what hit you!"

"Come on, Wallace," said the smaller man. "Leave 'em alone and let's go."

Astro took another step forward and roared, "Blast off. Both of you!"

The two men turned quickly and disappeared through the door leading to the next monorail car.

The three cadets turned and headed back down the aisle to their seats.

"Let's get some sleep," said Tom. "We better be in good shape for that new assignment when we hit the Academy. No telling what it'll be, where we'll go, or worse yet, when we'll blast off. And I, for one, want to have a good night's rest under my belt."

"Yeah," agreed Roger, settling himself into the cushions once more. "Wonder what the orders will be. Got any ideas, Tom?"

"No idea at all, Roger," answered Tom. "The audiogram just said report back to the Academy immediately for assignment."

"Hey, Astro!" exclaimed Roger, seeing the Venusian climb back into his seat. "Aren't you going to eat?"

"I'm not hungry any more," grunted Astro. "Those guys made me lose my appetite."

Tom looked at Roger and winked. "Maybe we'd better tell

Captain Strong about this, Roger."

"Why?"

"Get Astro mad enough and he won't want to eat. The Academy can cut down on its food bills."

"Ah, rocket off, you guys," growled Astro sleepily.

Tom and Roger smiled at each other, closed their eyes, and in a moment the three cadets of the Polaris unit were sound asleep.

* * * * *

Suspended from a single gleaming rail that stretched across the western plains like an endless silver ribbon, the monorail express hurtled through the early dawn speeding its passengers to their destination. As the gleaming line of streamlined cars crossed the newly developed grazing lands that had once been the great American desert, Tom Corbett stirred from a deep sleep. The slanting rays of the morning sun were shining in his eyes. Tom yawned, stretched, and turned to the viewport to watch the scenery flash past. Looming up over the flat grassy plains ahead, he could see a huge bluish mountain range, its many peaks covered with ever-present snow. In a few moments Tom knew the train would rocket through a tunnel and then on the other side, in the center of a deep, wide valley, he would see Space Academy, the university of the planets and headquarters of the great Solar Guard.

He reached over and shook Roger and Astro, calling, "All right, spacemen, time to hit the deck!"

"Uh? Ah-ummmh!" groaned Roger.

"Ahhhoooohhhhhh!" yawned Astro. Standing up, he stretched and touched the top of the monorail car.

"Let's get washed before the other passengers wake up," said Tom, and headed for the morning room. Astro and Roger followed, dragging their feet and rubbing their eyes.

Five minutes later, as the sleek monorail whistled into the tunnel beneath the mountain range, the boys of the *Polaris* unit returned to their seats.

"Back to the old grind," sighed Roger. "Drills, maneuvers, books, lectures. The same routine, day in day out."

"Maybe not," said Tom. "Remember, the order for us to report back was signed by Commander Walters, not the cadet supervisor of leaves. I think that means something special."

Suddenly the monorail roared out of the tunnel and into brilliant early-morning sun again.

The three cadets turned quickly, their eyes sweeping the valley for the first sight of the shining Tower of Galileo.

"There it is," said Tom, pointing toward a towering crystal building reflecting the morning light. "We'll be there in a minute."

Even as Tom spoke, the speed of the monorail slackened as it eased past a few gleaming structures of aluminum and concrete. Presently the white platform of the Academy station drifted past the viewport and all forward motion stopped. The doors opened and the three boys hurried to the exit.

All around the cadets, men and women in the vari-colored uniforms of the Solar Guard hurried through the station. The green of the Earthworm cadets, first-year students of the Cadet Corps; the brilliant rich blue of the senior cadets like the *Polaris* unit; the scarlet red of the enlisted Solar Guard; and here and there, the black and gold of the officers of the Solar Guard.

The three cadets hurried to the nearest slidewalk, a moving belt of plastic that glided silently across the ground toward Space Academy. It whisked them quickly past the few buildings nestled around the monorail station and rounded a curve. The three cadets looked up together at the gleaming Tower of Galileo. Made of pure Titan crystal, it soared above the cluster of buildings that surrounded the grassy quadrangle and dominated Space Academy like a translucent giant.

The cadets stepped off the slidewalk as it glided past the Tower building and ran up the broad marble stair. At the huge main portal, Tom stopped and looked back over the Academy grounds. All around him lay the evidence of mankind's progress. It was the year 2353, when Earthman had long since colonized the inner planets, Mars and Venus, and the three large satellites, Moon of Earth, Ganymede of Jupiter, and Titan of Saturn. It was the age of space travel; of the Solar Alliance, a unified society of billions of people who lived in peace with one another, though sprawled throughout the universe; and the Solar Guard, the might of the Solar Alliance and the defender of interplanetary peace. All these things Tom saw as he stood in the wide portal of the Tower Building, flanked by Astro and Roger.

Turning into the Tower, the three cadets went directly to the office of their unit commander. The training program at Space Academy consisted of three cadets to a unit, with a Solar

Guard officer as their teacher and instructor. Steve Strong, captain in the Solar Guard, had been their cadet instructor since the unit had been formed and he now smiled a welcome as the cadets snapped to attention in front of his desk.

"*Polaris* unit reporting as ordered, sir," said Tom, handing over the audiogram order he had received the day before.

"Thank you, Corbett," said Strong, taking the paper. "At ease."

The three boys relaxed and broke into wide grins as Strong rounded his desk and shook hands with each of them.

"Glad to have you back, boys," he said. "Did you enjoy your leave?"

"And how, sir," replied Tom.

"Tom's mother showed us a whale of a good time," chimed in Roger.

"And how she can cook!" Astro licked his lips involuntarily.

"Well, I hope you had a good rest—" said Strong, but was suddenly interrupted by the sound of a small bell. Behind his desk a small teleceiver screen glowed into life to reveal the stern face of Commander Walters, the commander of Space Academy.

Strong turned to the teleceiver and called, "Yes, Commander Walters?"

"Did the *Polaris* unit arrive yet, Steve?" asked the commander.

"Yes, sir," replied Strong. "They're here in my office now, sir."

"Good," said the commander with a smile. "I just received a report the exposition will open sooner than expected. I suggest you brief the cadets and raise ship as soon as possible."

"Very well, sir," answered Strong. The screen darkened and he turned back to the cadets. "Looks like you got back just in time."

"What's up, sir?" asked Tom.

Strong returned to his chair and sat down. "I suppose you've all heard about the Solar Exposition that opens on Venus next week?"

Tom's eyes lit up. "Have we! That's all the stereos and visunews and teleceivers have been yacking about for weeks now."

"Well," said Strong with a smile, "we're going!"

The three cadets couldn't restrain themselves and burst out in a happy shout. Then Roger calmed down enough to comment, "Sounds more like another vacation than an assignment, sir."

"Hardly, Manning," replied Strong. "You see, every industry, society, organization, and governmental agency is setting up exhibits at the exposition to show the people what's taking place in their part of the solar system. There'll also be an amusement section." Strong chuckled. "I've seen pictures of some of the tricks and rides they've developed to entertain the younger generation. Believe me, I'd rather take full acceleration on a rocket ship than ride on any of them."

"But what will we do, sir?" asked Tom.

"Our job is very simple. We're to take the *Polaris* to the exposition and land on the fairgrounds. When the fair opens, we show all the visitors who are interested, everything about her."

"You mean we're going to be"—Roger swallowed— "guides?"

"That's right, Manning," said Strong. "You three will guide all visitors through the *Polaris*."

"How long will we be there, sir?" asked Tom.

"A month or so, I guess. The *Polaris* will be the first Academy exhibit. When you leave, another unit will replace you with their ship and do the same thing."

"But—but—" stammered Astro, "what will we say to them? The visitors, I mean?"

"Just answer all their questions, Astro. Also, make up a little speech about the functions of your particular station."

Strong looked at his watch and rose to his feet. "It's getting late. Check the *Polaris* over and stand by to raise ship in an hour."

"Yes, sir," said Tom.

The cadets came to attention, preparing to leave.

"One thing more! Don't get the idea that this is going to be a space lark," said Strong. "It's very important for the people of the Solar Alliance to know what kind of work we're doing here at the Academy. And you three have been selected as representatives of the entire Cadet Corps. So see that you conduct yourselves accordingly. All right, dismissed!"

The three cadets saluted sharply and filed out of the room, their skipper's final words ringing in their ears.

Fifteen minutes later, having packed the necessary gear for the extended trip, the *Polaris* unit rode the slidewalk through the grassy quadrangle and the cluster of Academy buildings, out toward the spaceport. In the distance they could see the rocket cruiser *Polaris*, poised on the launching ramp, her long silhouette outlined sharply against the blue sky. Resting on her four stabilizer fins, her nose pointed toward the stars, the ship looked like a giant projectile poised and ready to blast its target.

"Look at her!" exclaimed Astro. "If she isn't the most beautiful ship in the universe, I'll eat my hat."

"Don't see how you could," drawled Roger, "after the way you put away Mrs. Corbett's pies!"

Tom laughed. "I'll tell you one thing, Roger," he said, pointing to the ship, "I feel like that baby is as much my home as Mom's and Dad's house back in New Chicago."

"All right, all right," said Roger. "Since we're all getting sloppy, I have to admit that I'm glad to see that old thrust bucket too!"

Presently the three cadets were scrambling into the mighty spaceship, and they went right to work, preparing for blast-off.

Quickly, with sure hands, each began a systematic check of his station. On the power deck Astro, a former enlisted Solar Guardsman who had been admitted to the Cadet Corps because of his engineering genius, stripped to the waist and started working on the ship's massive atomic engines. A heavy rocketman's belt of tools slung around his waist, he crawled through the heart of the ship, adjusting a valve here, turning a screw there, seeing that the reactant feeders were clean and clear to the rocket firing chambers. And last of all he made sure the great rocket firing chambers were secure and the heavy sheets of lead baffling in place to protect him from deadly radioactivity.

On the radar bridge in the nose of the ship, Roger removed the delicate astrogation prism from its housing and cleaned it with a soft cloth. Replacing it carefully, he turned to the radar scanner, checking the intricate wiring system and making sure that the range finders were in good working order. He then turned his attention to the intercom.

"Radar bridge to control deck," he called. "Checking the intercom, Tom."

Immediately below, on the control deck, Tom turned away from the control panel. "All clear here, Roger. Check with Astro."

"All clear on the power deck!" The big Venusian's voice boomed over the loud-speaker. The intercom could be heard all over the ship unless the many speakers were turned off individually.

Tom turned his attention back to the great control panel, and one by one tested the banks of dials, gauges, and indicators that controlled the rocket cruiser. Tom Corbett had wanted to be a space Cadet as long as he could remember. After taking the entrance exams, he had been accepted for the rigid training that would prepare him to enter the ranks of the great Solar Guard. He had met his two unit-mates, Roger and Astro, on his very first day at the Academy, and after a difficult beginning, adjusting to each other's personalities and the discipline of the Academy routine, the three boys had become steadfast friends.

As control-deck cadet and pilot, Tom was head of the unit, second-in-command to Captain Strong. And while he could issue orders to Astro and Roger and expect to be obeyed, the three cadets all spoke their minds when it came to making difficult decisions. This had solidified the three cadets into a fighting, experienced, dependable unit.

Tom made a final check on the gravity generator and turned to the intercom.

"All departments, report!" he called.

"Radar bridge checks in O.K.," replied Roger.

"Power deck checks in on the nose, Tom," reported Astro.

"Right! Stand by! We blast as soon as the skipper gets around."

Tom turned to the teleceiver and switched it on. The screen blurred and then steadied into a view of the spaceport outside. Tom scanned the launching ramp below, and, satisfied it was clear, he switched the teleceiver to the spaceport traffic-control circuit.

"Rocket cruiser *Polaris* to spaceport control," he called. "Come in, spaceport control. Request orbit clearance."

"Spaceport traffic control to *Polaris*," reported the traffic officer, his face in focus on the teleceiver screen. "Your orbit has been cleared for blast-off. Orbit number 3847—repeat, 3847—raise ship when ready!"

"Orbit 3847," repeated Tom. "End transmission!"

"End transmission," said the officer. Tom flipped off the teleceiver and the officer's face disappeared.

At the rear of the control deck, Captain Strong suddenly stepped through the hatch and dropped his black plastic space bag on the deck. Tom got up and saluted sharply.

"*Polaris* ready to blast off, sir," he said. "Orbit cleared."

"Very well, Corbett," replied Strong, returning the salute. "Carry on!"

Tom turned back to the control board and flipped on the intercom. "Control deck to power deck! Energize the cooling pumps!"

"Cooling pumps, aye!" said Astro.

From the power deck, the massive pumps began their whining roar. The great ship shuddered under the pressure.

Tom watched the gauge that indicated the pressure control and then called into the intercom.

"Radar bridge, do we have a clear trajectory?'

"All clear forward and up, Tom," reported Roger from the radar bridge.

"Strap in for blast-off!" bawled the curly-haired cadet.

Captain Strong took his place in the pilot's chair next to Tom and strapping himself in snapped out, "Feed reactant!"

Spinning a small wheel at the side of the control panel, Tom reported, "Feeders at D-9 rate, sir!"

Then, as the hiss of fuel pouring into the mighty engines of the ship blended with the whine of the pumps, Tom snapped out a third order. "Cut in take-off six yards!"

Receiving acknowledgment from below, he grasped the master blast-off switch and watched the sweeping hand of the astral chronometer.

"Stand by to raise ship!" he yelled. "Blast off minus—five—four—three—two—one—*zero*!"

He pulled the switch.

Slowly, the rockets blasting evenly, the giant ship lifted itself free of the ground. Then, gaining speed, it began rocketing away from the Earth. Like a giant shining bullet, the great spaceship blasted through the dark void of space, her nose pointed to the distant misty planet of Venus.

Once again Tom Corbett and his unit-mates had embarked on a mission for the Solar Guard.

Carey Rockwell

CHAPTER 2

"Stand by for touchdown!" bellowed Captain Strong's voice on the big spaceship's intercom.

"Control deck standing by," replied Tom.

"Corbett," Strong continued, "you may take her down as soon as you get clearance from Venusport traffic control."

Tom acknowledged the order with a brisk "Aye, sir! In a few moments he received permission to touch down on the newly colonized planet. Then, turning his attention to the control board, he requested a ground-approach check from Roger.

"About two miles to touchdown, Tom," reported Roger from the radar bridge. "Trajectory clear!"

"O.K., Roger," said Tom. Glancing quickly at the air speed and rocket thrust indicators, he flipped a switch and sang out, "Power deck, reduce thrust on main drive rockets to minimum!"

"Got ya, Tom," boomed Astro.

"Closing in fast, sir," said Tom to Strong, who had come up from below and now stood at the cadet's shoulder watching as Tom maneuvered the big ship through the Venusian atmosphere, his keen eyes sweeping the great panel of recording gauges and dials.

"One thousand feet to touchdown," intoned Roger from the radar bridge.

Reacting swiftly, Tom adjusted several levers, then picking up the intercom microphone, he threw a switch and yelled, "Power deck! Full braking thrust!"

Deep inside the *Polaris*, Astro, who tended the mighty rocket power plant with loving care, eased home the sensitive control mechanism, applying even pressure to the braking rockets.

As the giant spaceship settled smoothly to within a few feet of the surface of the concrete spaceport, Tom threw the master switch that cut all power. A moment later the huge craft dropped easily, then settled on the landing platform with a gentle thump.

"Touchdown!" yelled Tom. Then, glancing at the astral chronometer on the control board, he turned to Strong, and saluting smartly, reported, "*Polaris* completes space flight at exactly seven fifty-two-O-two!"

Strong returned the salute. "Very well, Tom. Now, I want you, Roger, and Astro to come with me to the exposition commissioner's office for an interview and detailed orders."

"Yes, sir," said Tom.

A few minutes later, dressed in fresh uniforms, the three cadets followed their unit commander out of the ship, then stood by as Strong ordered the chief petty officer of an enlisted Solar Guard working party to prepare the *Polaris* for moving to the exposition site.

"Empty the reactant fuel tanks of all but enough for us to raise ship and touch down over to the fairgrounds," said Strong. "Better strip her of armament, too. Paralo-ray pistols and rifles, the three-inch and six-inch atomic blasters, narco sleeping gas; in fact, everything that could possibly cause any trouble."

"Yes, sir," replied the scarlet-clad enlisted spaceman.

"One thing more," added Strong. "There will be a crew living aboard, so please see that the galley is stocked with a full supply of both fresh and synthetic foods. That's about all, I guess."

"Very well, sir," replied the petty officer with a crisp salute. He turned and began bawling orders to a squad of men behind him and immediately they were swarming over the great ship like ants.

Fifteen minutes later, a jet cab swerved to a stop in front of the tallest of the Venusport buildings, the Solar Alliance Chamber. Strong paid the driver, adding a handsome tip, and flanked by his three cadets strode briskly into the building.

Crossing a high-ceilinged lobby, they entered an express vacuum elevator and five seconds later stepped out onto the four-hundredth floor. There, Strong slid a panel door to one side, and, followed by the cadets, stepped inside the office of Mike Hawks, exposition commissioner and retired senior officer of the Solar Guard.

The office was impressively large and airy, with an outside wall forming a viewport of clear Titan crystal reaching from floor to vaulted ceiling and affording a magnificent view of the city of Venusport and, beyond it, the futuristic buildings of the exposition itself. Another wall, equally as large, was covered by a map of the exposition grounds.

Mike Hawks, a man with steel-gray hair, clear blue eyes, and a ramrod military bearing, sat behind a massive desk talking to two men. He looked up when Strong and the cadets walked in and rose quickly with a broad smile to greet them.

"Steve!" he exclaimed, rounding the desk to shake hands with his old friend. "I never dreamed we'd have you and the *Polaris* unit at our fair!" He nodded warmly to the cadets who stood at rigid attention. "At ease, cadets. Glad to have you aboard."

"I was just as surprised to get this assignment, Mike," said Strong, pumping the officer's hand. Nodding toward the men seated in front of Hawks' desk, he apologized, "Sorry to bust in on you like this, old man. Didn't know you were busy."

"It's quite all right." The commissioner smiled. "Just handing out a few licenses for the concessions in the amusement section at the fair. People expect to have a little fun when they go to a fair, you know. By the stars, they're going to have it so long as I'm commissioner." He turned to the cadets. "Sit down, boys. You too, Steve. I'll be with you in a minute." He turned back to his desk and the waiting men.

The cadets, at a nod from Strong, sat down on a leather couch that stretched the length of one wall and listened while Hawks completed his business with the two men.

"There you are," said Hawks, applying the seal of his office to a slip of paper. "That gives you the right to operate a concession in the amusement area as long as the fair is open."

Carey Rockwell

One of the men took the paper and glanced at it quickly.

"Wait a minute, Commissioner. This is over near the edge of the area," he complained. "We wanted to get in the middle. How do you expect us to make any credits away out there by ourselves?" The man's tone was surly and disrespectful.

"Sorry, but that's the only location left. In fact," Hawks added acidly, "you're lucky to get it!"

"Really?" sneered the heavier of the two. "Well, I'm sure going to find out about this!"

Hawks stood up and eyed the two men coldly. "I've been appointed commissioner of this exposition by the delegates to the Solar Alliance Council. I answer only to the council. If you have a complaint, then you must present your case before that body." He cleared his throat and glared at them from behind his desk. "Good day, gentlemen!" he said.

The two men, who until now had been seated facing the desk, got up, and after glaring at Hawks, turned and walked toward the door. Tom gasped, and grabbing Roger by the arm, involuntarily pointed at the two men.

"Look, Roger—those men—" he whispered.

"Yeah," said Roger. "Those are the wise-guy space crawlers we met on the monorail, the ones who called us punks!"

"How'd they get here so fast?" asked Astro.

"Must have taken a jetliner from Atom City, I guess."

Strong, who sat near Tom, heard the exchange between the cadets.

"You know those men?" he asked.

"Well—uh—not exactly, sir. We just had a little run-in with them on the monorail returning from leave, that's all," said Tom. "Nothing serious. They don't think much of the Solar Guard, though."

"I gathered as much," said Hawks dryly. He walked over from his desk. "I hated to give them the license to operate, but I had to, since I had no valid reason to turn them down. They have a good idea, too."

"That so? What is it?" asked Strong.

"They have an old chemical-burning space freighter in which they're going to take fair visitors up for a short ride. You see, the big one, Gus Wallace, is an old deep-space merchantman. The smaller one is Luther Simms, a rocketman."

"Hm. Not a bad idea at all," mused Strong. "They should make out all right."

With that, the two Solar Guard officers dropped the incident of Wallace and Simms and turned to exchanging news of mutual friends and of what each had been doing since their last meeting. Finally, as the conversation was brought around to the exposition, Hawks got up and sat on the side of the desk, facing Strong and the cadets. His eyes glowed as he spoke.

"Steve," he said, "this is going to be the greatest gathering of minds, thoughts, and ideas in the knowledgeable history of mankind! There are going to be lectures from the greatest minds in the system on any and all subjects you can think of. In one building we're going to build a whole spaceship—a rocket cruiser—piece by piece, right in front of the eyes of

Carey Rockwell

fair visitors. In another building we're going to have the greatest collection of musicians in the universe, continuously playing the most beautiful music, in a hall built to seat a half million people. Industry, science, medicine, art, literature, astrophysics, space flight, to say nothing of a comparative history exhibit designed to show the people where our forefathers went off the track by warring against each other. In fact, Steve, everything you can think of, and then more, will be represented here at the exposition. Why, do you know I've been working for three years, co-ordinating ideas, activity, and information!"

Strong and the cadets sat transfixed as they listened to the commissioner speak in glowing terms of the exposition, which, until this time, by the cadets at least, had been considered little more than a giant amusement park. Finally Strong managed to say, "And we thought the *Polaris* was going to be so big, it'd be the center of attraction." He smiled.

Hawks waved his hand. "Look, I don't want to offend you or the boys, Steve, but the fact is, the *Polaris* is one of the *smaller* exhibits!"

"I can see that now," answered Strong. "Tell me, Mike, just what do you want us to do?"

"I'll answer that in two parts. First, I would like the cadets to set up the *Polaris*, get her shining and bright, and with quiet courtesy, answer any question anyone might ask concerning the ship, referring any question they can't answer to the information center in the Space Building."

"That's all, sir?" asked Tom incredulously.

"That's all, Corbett. You open the *Polaris* at nine in the

morning and close her at nine at night. You'll be living aboard, of course."

"Yes, sir. Of course, sir."

"That sounds so simple," drawled Roger, "it might be tough."

"It will be tough, Manning," commented Hawks. "Don't fool yourself into assuming otherwise."

"Don't worry about these boys, Mike. Now, what is part two?" Strong asked.

Hawks smiled. "Here it is, Steve. The Solar Alliance has decided to open the exposition with a simple speech made by a relatively unknown person, but one who is deserving of such an honor. They left the choice of that person up to me." He paused and added quietly, "I'd like you to make that opening speech, Steve."

"Me!" cried Strong. "Me, make a speech?"

"I can't think of anyone more deserving—or dependable."

"But—but—" stammered the captain, "I can't make a speech. I wouldn't know what to say."

"Say anything you want. Just make it short and to the point."

Strong hesitated a moment. He realized it was a great honor, but his naturally shy personality kept him from accepting.

"Steve, it may make it easier for you to know," said Hawks teasingly, "that there's going to be a giant capsule lowered into the ground which will contain a record of every bit of progress made since the inception of the Solar Alliance. It's designed to show the men of the future how to do everything from treating a common cold to exploding nuclear power. This capsule will be lowered at the end of your opening address. So, most of the attention will be focused on the capsule, not you." The commissioner smiled.

"All right, Mike," said Strong, grinning sheepishly. "You've got yourself a speechmaker!"

"Good!" said Hawks and the two men shook hands.

Tom Corbett could contain himself no longer. "Congratulations, sir!" he blurted out as the three cadets stood up. "We think Commissioner Hawks couldn't have made a better choice!" His unit-mates nodded a vigorous assent.

Strong shook hands with the cadets and thanked them.

"You want the cadets for anything right now, Mike?" asked Strong.

"Not a thing, Steve."

Strong turned back to the boys. "Better hop out to the spaceport and get the *Polaris* over the exposition site, cadets. Soon as you set her down, clean her up a little, then relax. I'll be at the Galaxy Hotel if you need me."

"Yes, sir," said Tom.

The cadets saluted sharply and left the office.

Arriving at the spaceport, they found the *Polaris* stripped of her guns and her galley stocked with food. The chief petty officer in charge of the enlisted spacemen detail was roving through the passageways of the rocket cruiser when Tom found him.

"Everything set, chief?" asked Tom.

"All set, Cadet Corbett," reported the elderly spaceman, saluting smartly. He gave Tom a receipt for the list of the equipment that had been removed from the ship and signed the logbook. Tom thanked him and made a hurried check of the control deck, with Roger and Astro reporting from the radar and power decks. With the precision and assurance of veteran spacemen, the three Space Cadets lifted the great ship up over the heart of the sprawling Venusian city and brought it down gently in the clearing provided for it at the exposition site, a grassy square surrounded on three sides by buildings of shimmering crystal walls.

No sooner had the giant ship settled itself to the ground, than a crew of exposition workers began laying a slidewalk toward her, while another crew began the construction of an aluminum staircase to the entrance port in her giant fin.

Almost before they realized it, Tom, Roger, and Astro found themselves busy with a hundred little things concerning the ship and their part in the fair. They were visited by the subcommissioner of the exposition and advised of the conveniences provided for the participants of the fair. Then, finally, as a last worker finished the installation of a photoelectric cell across the entrance port to count visitors to the ship, Tom, Roger, and Astro began the dirty job of washing down the giant titanium hull with a special cleaning fluid, while all around them the activity of the fair buzzed with nervous excitement.

Suddenly the three cadets heard the unmistakable roar of jets in the sky. Automatically, they looked up and saw a spaceship, nose up, decelerating as it came in for a touchdown on a clearing across one of the wide spacious streets of the fairgrounds.

"Well, blast my jets!" exclaimed Astro, his eyes clinging to the flaming exhausts as the ship lowered itself to the ground.

"That craft must be at least fifty years old!"

"I've got a rocket-blasting good idea, Tom," said Roger.

The exit port of the spaceship opened, and the three cadets watched Gus Wallace and Luther Simms climb down the ladder.

"Hey," yelled Roger, "better be careful with that broken-down old boiler. It might blow up!"

The two men glared at the grinning Roger but didn't answer.

"Take it easy, Roger," cautioned Tom. "We don't want to start anything that might cause us and Captain Strong trouble before the fair even opens. So let's leave them alone."

"What are you afraid of?" drawled Roger, a mischievous gleam in his eyes. "Just a little fun with those guys won't hurt." He stepped to the side of the clearing and leaned over the fence separating the two areas.

"Tell me something, spaceman," he yelled to Wallace, who was busy with some gear at the base of the ship, "you don't expect people to pay to ride that thing, do you?" He smiled derisively and added, "Got insurance to cover the families?"

"Listen, punk!" sneered Wallace, "get back over to your Solar Guard space toy and keep your trap shut!"

"Now—now—" jeered Roger, "mustn't get nasty. Remember, we're going to be neighbors. Never can tell when you might want to borrow some baling wire or chewing gum to keep your craft together!"

"Look, wise guy, one more crack out of you, and I'll send you out of this world without a spaceship!" snarled Wallace through grating teeth.

"Any time you'd like to try that, you know where I am," Roger snapped back.

"Okay, punk! You asked for it," yelled Wallace. He had been holding a length of chain and now he swung it at Roger. The cadet ducked easily, hopped over the fence, and before Wallace knew what was happening, jolted him with three straight lefts and a sharp right cross. Wallace went down in a heap, out cold.

Luther Simms, who had been watching the affair from one side, now rushed at Roger with a monkey wrench. With the ferocity of a bull, Astro roared at the small spaceman, who stopped as if pulled up by a string. Roger spun around, made an exaggerated bow, and smiling, asked, "Next?"

At this point, aware that things were getting a bit thick, Tom strode across the clearing, and grabbing the still smiling Roger, pulled him away.

"Are you space happy?" he asked, "You know you goaded him into swinging that chain, Roger. And that makes you entirely responsible for what just happened!"

"Yeah," growled Astro. "Suppose he had hit you with it, then what?"

Roger, still grinning, glanced over his shoulder and saw Simms helping Wallace to his feet. He turned to Astro, threw his arm over the big cadet's shoulder, and drawled, "Why, then you'd have just taken them apart to avenge me! Wouldn't you, pal?"

"Aw, stow it," snapped Tom. For a second Roger looked at him sharply, then broke into a smile again. "O.K., Tom, I'm sorry," he said. "O.K., let's get back to work," ordered Tom.

Back at the *Polaris*, as they continued cleaning the hull of the ship, Tom saw the two men disappear into their craft, throwing dirty looks back at the three cadets as they went.

"You know, Roger, I think you made a very bad mistake," he said. "One way or another, they'll try to even the score with you."

"And it won't be just a report to Captain Strong," added Astro darkly.

Roger, cocky and unafraid, broke out his engaging grin again and shrugged his shoulders.

CHAPTER 3

"... And so we dedicate this capsule to the civilizations of the future. Those who may dig this cylinder out of the ground in ages to come will find within it the tools, the inventions, and the scientific wonders which have made the era of the Solar Alliance one of peace and lasting prosperity."

Captain Steve Strong paused, glanced at the huge crane and the shimmering steel capsule that dangled at the end of a cable, then called out, "Lower the capsule!"

The cheers of a hundred thousand people massed in the exposition plaza greeted the order. The stereo camera and teleceiver scanners that were sending the opening ceremonies of the Solar Exposition to all parts of the Alliance moved in to focus on the capsule as it was lowered into a deep, concrete-lined pit.

The three members of the *Polaris* unit, standing to one side of the platform, joined in the cheers as their skipper shook hands with the delegates and waved again and again at the roaring crowd.

"That was some speech, Tom," commented Roger. "I wonder who wrote it for him?"

Carey Rockwell

"He wrote it himself, Roger," replied Tom.

"Ah, go on," scoffed Roger.

"Sure he did," said Astro indignantly. "He sweated over it for nearly a week."

"Here he comes," said Tom. The three cadets watched Captain Strong, resplendent in his dress gold-and-black uniform, fight his way off the platform, shaking hands with congratulating strangers along the way.

"Congratulations, Captain Strong," said Tom with a smile.

"That was swell!" Roger and Astro chorused their agreement.

"Thanks, boys," gasped Strong. "But let me tell you, I never want to do that again. I was never so scared in my life!"

"Just making a speech?" asked Roger. "After all the lectures you've given at Space Academy?"

"They weren't before teleceiver and stereo cameras." Strong laughed. "Do you realize this ceremony is being seen on Mars, Earth, and all the colonized moons, clear out to Titan."

"Wow!" breathed Astro. "That would make me tongue-tied!"

"Huh! All that to stick a metal box into the ground," snorted Roger.

"It's not the capsule, Roger," said Tom. "It's what's inside the capsule."

"Right, Tom," said Strong. "Inside that capsule scientists have packed the whole history of man's march through the stars. They've included scientific formulas, medical, cultural, and industrial facts. Everything we know. Even some things that are known by only a handful of the most trusted men in the universe!" Strong stopped suddenly and laughed. "There I go, making another speech! Come on. Let's get out of here," he cried.

"Do we start showing people through the *Polaris* now, sir?" asked Astro.

"In the morning, Astro," replied Strong. "Tonight there's a big Solar Alliance banquet. You three are invited, too."

"Er—" stammered Roger, "you mean—a banquet—with—uh—?"

Strong laughed. "More speeches? I'm afraid so, Manning. Of course there'll be plenty of food."

"Well, it's not that we're against speeches," ventured Astro.

"Not yours anyway, sir," added Tom hastily. "But what we mean, sir, is that—"

Strong held up his hand. "I understand perfectly. Suppose you stay here on the exposition grounds. Have a look around. See the sights, have some fun."

"Yes, sir!" The boys chorused their reply.

"Just don't spend all your credits at the first booth," continued Strong. "And watch that Venusian cloud candy. It's good, but murder on the Earthman's stomach."

"Captain Strong!" A voice called from the platform above. It was one of the Venusian delegates. "They want some pictures of you!"

"Be right there, sir," replied Strong. He turned to the boys and smiled. "You're lucky you don't have to go through this. See you aboard ship later." Spinning quickly on his heel, he made his way back through the crowd to the platform.

"What a great guy," sighed Tom.

"Sure is," agreed Astro.

"Well, fellas," announced Roger, "we've got twelve hours liberty and a small scale model of the whole solar system to have fun in! What're we waiting for?"

Fighting their way through the crowds in the plaza, the three boys finally reached the amusement area where they wandered among gaily colored booths and plastic tents, their eyes lighting up with each new attraction.

Two hours later, stuffed with spaceburgers and Martian water, their arms loaded with assorted prizes, won by Astro's prowess in the weight-lifting booth, Tom's skill as a marksman, and Roger's luck at the wheels of chance, the cadets wearily returned to the Polaris.

As they neared their section of the fair site they heard a harsh voice appealing to a small crowd around the stand in front of Wallace and Simms' spaceship. A huge sign spelled out the attraction: RIDE IN SPACE—ONE CREDIT.

Luther Simms, a bamboo cane in one hand, a roll of tickets in another, was hawking his attraction to the bystanders.

"Step right up, ladies and gentlemen! Step right up! It's a thrill of a lifetime, the greatest sensation of the entire exposition. Ride a rocket ship, and all this for one credit! A lone, single credit, ladies and gents, will buy you a pathway to the stars! Step right up—"

In laughing groups, the crowd around the stand began to purchase tickets and climb aboard the old freighter.

The three cadets watched from the outer edge of the crowd.

"Hey, fellas," said Roger suddenly, "whaddya say we go?"

"What?" gulped Astro. "On that thing?"

"Why not?" urged Roger.

"But that hulk should have been shipped back to the scrap furnace years ago!" Tom protested.

"So what, Junior?" drawled Roger. "Scared?"

"Don't be silly," replied Tom. "But with all the other things to do here, why should we—"

"Oh," said Astro, nudging Tom, "now I get it!"

"You get what?" asked Roger innocently.

"Those girls," said Astro. "They're just climbing aboard."

Glancing at the air lock, Tom saw three young and pretty girls file into the ship. "Oh, so that's it, huh?" he said, looking quizzically at his unit-mate.

The blond cadet's eyes were wide with mock surprise.

"Girls? Well, what do you know about that? I never noticed!"

"Yeah, I'll bet you didn't!" said Tom.

"Well, they *are* trim little space dolls. And there are three of them!"

"Come on, Astro," sighed Tom. "We have to give the little boy his fun."

They walked toward the stand where Simms was still making his pitch to the crowd.

"Just five more seats left, ladies and gentlemen, only five chances to blast into space ..."

Tom stepped up and put three credits on the counter. "Three, please," he said.

Simms looked down and suddenly stopped his harangue. His eyes narrowed with suspicion as he saw the three cadets standing before him. Hesitating, he glanced around, seemingly looking for help. Then, shrugging his shoulders, he handed over the tickets and turned to the crowd. "Three tickets for the Space Cadets, who live out there in space. Just can't stay away from it, eh, boys?"

"I only hope that tub of yours holds together," said Tom.

Simms snarled out of the side of his mouth, "Shut up, wise guy!" And then continued aloud, "Yes, Space Cadet, I agree with you. Everyone should take a trip into space."

Tom started to protest, but then shrugged his shoulders and followed Roger and Astro into the ship. On the stand, Simms continued his appeal to the crowd.

"Just two more tickets left, ladies and gentlemen! Who'll be the lucky two?"

Suddenly Gus Wallace appeared from behind the ship and approached the stand, calling, "Hey, Simms!"

Simms stopped speaking and turned to his partner. "Yeah?"

"Everything's all set. Let's blast off!"

"I'll be with you as soon as I sell the last two tickets," said Simms. "Here you are, ladies and gents, the last two—"

Wallace grabbed him by the arm and yanked him from the stand. "I said we blast off, you idiot! You want to risk everything for two lousy credits?"

"O.K., O.K. Don't blow a fuse!"

Simms quickly closed the stand, turned out the lighted sign, and followed Wallace into the old freighter. He then collected the tickets and made sure all the passengers were strapped into their acceleration chairs and finally went below to the power deck. Wallace disappeared into the control room and seconds later his voice was heard over the ship's intercom gruffly announcing the blast-off. The lights in the cabin dimmed, the air was filled with a low whining hiss, and for an instant the old ship bucked and groaned. Suddenly, with a loud explosive roar, she blasted into the sky and began a sluggish arching climb into space.

"All right, fellas," said Roger, after the force of acceleration eased off, "let's try a little encircling maneuver on those girls up ahead."

"Oh, no, Roger," answered Tom. "You're flying solo on that project!"

"Yeah, you go ahead, Romeo." Astro laughed. "I'd like to see the Manning technique in action."

A loud explosion suddenly rocked the spaceship.

"What was that?" cried Roger. "Maybe this old tub won't make it after all!"

Astro smiled. "This is a chemical burner, remember? Her initial acceleration isn't enough. They have to keep blasting her to make speed."

"Oh, sure," drawled Roger, relaxing again and watching the girls ahead. "Well, here I go!" He got up and lurched down the aisle running between the seats.

"Hey there!" roared Simms, who had suddenly appeared at the power-deck hatch. "Keep your seat!"

"Who, me?" asked Roger.

"Not your Aunt Tilly, wise guy! Sit down and shut up!"

"Listen," said Roger, "you don't seem to realize—"

"I realize you're going to sit down or else!" snarled Simms.

Roger retreated to his seat and sat down. "Ah, go blast your jets," he grumbled as Simms continued up the aisle to the control deck.

Tom and Astro doubled over with laughter. "Welcome back, Roger," bellowed the big Venusian. "I don't think those girls are the sociable type, anyway."

"Wouldn't you know," moaned Roger, "that space creep had

to show up just when I had the whole campaign laid out in my mind." He gazed sadly at the pert heads of the girls in front of him.

Tom gave Astro a wink. "Poor Manning. All set to go hyperdrive and ran into space junk before he cleared atmosphere."

Suddenly another explosion racked the ship and the rockets cut out all together. The passengers began to look around nervously.

"By the craters of Luna, what was *that*?" demanded Tom, looking at Astro.

"The rockets have cut out," answered the Venusian. "Hope we're out in free fall, beyond the pull of Venus' gravity."

The forward hatch of the passenger cabin opened and Simms reappeared followed by Wallace.

"Take it easy, folks," said Wallace, "nothing to get excited about. We're in free fall, holding a course around the planet. So just sit back and enjoy the view!"

A chorus of sighs filled the cabin and the passengers began laughing and chatting again, pointing out various sights on the planet below them. Smiling, Wallace and Simms marched down the aisle. Suddenly Roger and Tom rose and blocked their path.

"What's up, Wallace?" demanded Tom.

Wallace gave the two boys a hard look. "So it's you, huh? You got a lot of nerve coming aboard this ship."

"If there's something wrong, Wallace," said Tom, "maybe we could give you a hand."

"Get back in your seats," ordered Wallace. "We don't need any cadet squirts getting in our way!"

"Why, you overweight space jockey," snapped Roger, "we know more about spaceships than you'll ever learn!"

"One more crack out of you and I'll blast your ears off!" roared Wallace. *"Now sit down!"*

Roger's face turned a deep red and he moved toward Wallace, but Tom put out a restraining hand.

"Take it easy, Roger," he said. "Wallace is the skipper of this boiler. In space he's the boss."

"You bet I'm the boss," snarled Wallace. "Now keep that loud-mouthed punk quiet, or I'll wipe up the deck with him and send the pieces back to Space Academy!"

"Hey, Wallace," yelled Simms, who had walked away when the argument started. "Come on. We gotta fix that reactor unit!"

"Yeah—yeah," Wallace called back. He turned to Roger again. "Just remember what I said, cadet!" Brushing the boys aside, he strode down the aisle to join Simms.

As the two men disappeared through the power-deck hatch, Tom turned to Roger and tried to calm him down. "Skippers are skippers, Roger, even aboard a piece of space junk!"

"Yeah," growled Roger, "but I don't like to be called a squirt or a punk! Why, I know more about reactor units than—"

"Reactor units?" broke in Astro from his seat.

"Yeah. Didn't you hear what Simms said?"

"But this is a chemical burner," said Astro. "Why an atomic reactor unit aboard?"

"Might be a booster for extra speed," offered Tom. "And more power."

"On a simple hop like this? Hardly out of the atmosphere?" Astro shook his head. "No, Tom. It doesn't make sense."

"Well," chimed in Roger, "here's something else I've been wondering about. They charge one credit for this ride. Which makes a total of about fifty credits for a capacity load—"

"I get you," Tom interrupted. "It costs at least two hundred credits in fuel alone to get one of these chemical jalopies off the ground!"

Roger looked at Tom solemnly. "You know, Tom, I'd certainly like to know what those guys are doing. You just don't hand out free rides in space."

"How about snooping around?" asked Astro.

Tom thought a moment. "O.K. You two stay here. I'll go aft and see what they're doing."

Tom walked quickly to the stern of the ship, entered the power-deck hatch, and disappeared. Astro and Roger, each taking one side of the ship, strained for a look from the viewports. In a few minutes Tom returned.

"Spot anything?" asked Roger.

"I'm not so sure," answered Tom. "They weren't on the power deck and the cargo hatch was locked. I looked out the stern viewport, but all I could see was a thick black cloud."

"Well, that's no help," said Roger. Suddenly the blond cadet snapped his fingers. "Tom, I'll bet they're smugglers!"

"What?" asked Tom.

"That's it," said Roger. "I'll bet that's it. The concession is just a phony to cover up their smuggling. It lets them take a load of stuff up without a custom's search. Then, when they're far enough out—"

"They dump it," supplied Astro.

"Right!" agreed Tom finally. "What better place to hide something than in space?"

"For someone else to pick up later!" added Roger triumphantly.

When Wallace and Simms returned, the three cadets were busy looking out the viewports. And later, when the spaceship was letting down over the exposition grounds, Tom commented on the ease with which the ship made her approach for a touchdown.

"Roger," asked Tom quietly, "notice how she's handling now?"

"How do you mean?" asked Roger.

"Going out," said Tom, "she wallowed like an old tub filled with junk. Now, while she's no feather, there's a big difference in the way she's maneuvering!"

"Then they did dump something in space!" said Roger.

"I'm sure of it!" said Tom. "And from now on, we're going to keep our eyes open and find out what it is!"

Carey Rockwell

CHAPTER 4

Tom glanced at the astral chronometer over the control board of the *Polaris* and sighed with relief. It was nine P.M. He turned to the intercom.

"Attention, please! Attention, please! The exhibit is now closing for the night. All visitors will kindly leave the ship immediately." He repeated the announcement again and turned to smile at the last lingering youngster ogling him before being yanked toward an exit by a tired and impatient mother.

The hatch to the radar bridge opened and Roger climbed down the ladder to flop wearily in the pilot's seat in front of the control panel.

"If one more scatterbrained female asks me how the astrogation prism works," groaned the blond cadet, "I'll give it to her and let her figure it out for herself!"

Astro joined them long enough to announce that he had made sandwiches and brewed hot chocolate. Tom and Roger followed him back to the galley.

Sipping the hot liquid, the three cadets looked at each other without speaking, each understanding what the other had been through. Even Astro, who normally would rather talk about his atomic engine than eat, confessed he was tired of explaining the functions of the reaction fuel force feed and the main valve of the cooling pumps.

"The worst of it is," sighed Astro, "they all pick on the same valve. What's so fascinating about one valve?"

Tom's job on the control deck was less tiring, since his was more of a command post, which demanded decisions, as conditions arose, rather than a fixed routine that could be explained. But even so, to be asked over and over what the astral chronometer was, how he could read time on Earth, Mars, Venus, Titan, Ganymede, and all the satellites at the same time was wearing on the toughest of young spirits.

Eager to forget the grueling day of questions and answers, the cadets turned their thoughts to the mysterious midnight activity that had been taking place around the spaceship concession during the last ten days.

"I just can't figure out what those guys are up to," said Roger, blowing on his hot chocolate. "We've watched those guys for over a week now and no one has even come near them with anything that could be smuggled."

"Could be a small package," suggested Astro, his mouth full of ham sandwich. "Somebody could take a ride and slip it to them."

"Hardly," said Tom. "Remember, that ship blasts off like she's loaded to the nose with cargo. And then she comes back like a feather. You can tell by the sound of her jets. So it wouldn't be anything small enough for someone to carry."

"Yeah, I guess you're right," agreed Astro.

"Well," said Tom finally, "I'm stumped. I think the only thing left to do is to decide if it's anything important enough to tell Captain Strong about. Working on the *Polaris* twelve hours a day and staying up all night to watch those two jokers has me all in."

Roger and Astro looked at each other and then silently nodded their agreement.

"O.K.," said Tom, "we'll go to the skipper's hotel in Venusport and tell him the whole thing. Let's see what he makes of it."

* * * * *

At that moment Captain Strong was in the office of Exposition Commissioner Mike Hawks trying to make sense out of a series of reports that had landed on the commissioner's desk. Hawks watched him carefully as he studied the papers.

"You say this is the ninth report you've received since the fair opened, Mike?" asked Strong finally.

Hawks nodded. He hadn't known whether to laugh off or seriously consider the nine space skippers' reports that the sky over the exposition site was dirty.

"Yes, Steve," he said. "That one came from the skipper of an express freighter. He blasted off this morning and ran through this so-called dirt. He thought it was just a freak of nature but reported it to be on the safe side."

"I don't suppose he took a sample of the stuff?"

"No. But I'm taking care of that," replied Hawks. "There's a rocket scout standing by right now. Want to come along?"

"Let me finish these reports first."

"Sure thing."

As Strong carefully checked each report, Commissioner Hawks rose and began to stride restlessly back and forth across the spacious office. He stopped in front of the window and stared out over the exposition grounds, watching the thousands of holiday visitors streaming in and out of the buildings, all unaware of the strange mystery in the sky above them. Hawks' attention was drawn to the giant solar beacon, a huge light that flashed straight out into space, changing color every second and sending out the message: "Quis separabit homo"—Who shall separate mankind?

This beacon that at the beginning of the exposition had reached into the black void of space like a clean bright ray was now cloudy and murky—the result of the puzzling "dirty sky."

"All right, Mike," Strong announced suddenly. "Let's go."

"Get anything more out of those reports?" asked Hawks, turning back to his desk.

"No," replied the Solar Guard officer. "They all tell the same story. Right after blast-off, the ships ran into a dirty sky."

"Sounds kind of crazy, doesn't it?"

"Crazy enough to check."

Hawks pressed a button on the desk intercom.

Carey Rockwell

"Yes, sir?" replied a metallic voice.

"Have the rocket scout ready for flight in five minutes," Hawks ordered. He snapped off the intercom without waiting for a reply and turned to Strong. "Let's go, Steve."

The two veteran spacemen left the office without further comment and rode down in the vacuum elevator to the highway level. Soon they were speeding out to the spaceport in Hawks' special jet car.

At the blast-pitted field they were met by a young Solar Guard officer and an elderly man carrying a leather case, who were introduced as Lieutenant Claude and Professor Newton.

While Claude prepared the rocket scout for blast-off, Strong, Hawks, and Newton discussed the possibility of lava dust having risen to great heights from another side of the planet.

"While I'm reasonably sure," stated Newton, "that no volcano has erupted recently here on Venus, I can't be sure until I've examined samples of this so-called dirt."

"I'll have Lieutenant Claude contact the University of Venus," said Hawks. "Their seismographs would pick up surface activity."

Claude stuck his head out of the hatch and reported the ship ready for blast-off. Strong followed the professor and Hawks aboard and strapped himself into an acceleration chair. In a moment they were blasting through the misty atmosphere of Venus into the depths of space.

Fifteen minutes later, Hawks and Strong were standing on the hull of the ship in space suits, watching the professor take a sample of a dirty black cloud, so thick it was impossible to see more than three feet. Strong called to the professor through the spacephone.

"What do you make of it, sir?" he asked.

"I wouldn't want to give you a positive opinion without chemical tests," answered the professor, his voice echoing in Strong's fish-bowl helmet. "But I believe it's one of three things. One, the remains of a large asteroid that has broken up. Two, volcanic ash, either from Venus or from Jupiter. But if it came from Jupiter, I don't see how it could have drifted this far without being detected on radar."

Now, holding a flask full of the black cloud, the professor started back to the air lock.

"You said three possibilities, professor," said Strong.

"The third," replied the professor, "could be—"

The professor was interrupted by Lieutenant Claude calling over the intercom.

"Just received a report from the University of Venus, sir!" said the young officer. "There's been no volcanic activity on Venus in the last ten years serious enough to create such a cloud."

Strong waited for the professor's reaction, but the elderly man was already entering the air lock. Before Strong and Hawks could catch up to him, the air-lock hatch slammed closed.

"Hey," exclaimed Strong, "what does he think he's doing?"

"Don't worry about it, Steve," replied Hawks. "He probably forgot we were out here with him, he's so concerned about this dirt. We'll just have to wait until he's out of the air lock."

The Solar Guard officer nodded, then looked around him at the thick black cloud that enveloped the ship. "Well," he said, "one of the professor's theories has been knocked out."

"Yes," replied Hawks. "Which means this stuff is either the remains of a large asteroid or—"

"The third possibility," finished Strong, "which the professor never explained."

Suddenly the air-lock hatch opened again and the two spacemen stepped inside. Closing the hatch behind them, they waited until the pressure was built up again to equal that of the ship, and then they removed their helmets and space suits.

Leaving the air lock and walking down the companionway, Hawks suddenly caught Strong by the arm.

"Have you considered the possibility of this cloud being radioactive, Steve?" he asked.

Strong nodded slowly. "That's all I've been thinking about since I first heard about it, Mike. I think I'd better report this to Commander Walters at Space Academy."

"Wait, Steve," said Hawks. "If you do that, Walters might close the exposition. Wait until you get a definite opinion from Professor Newton."

Strong considered a moment. "I guess a few more minutes won't make a lot of difference," he said finally. He realized how important the exposition was to his old friend. But at the same time, he knew what would happen if a radioactive cloud suddenly settled on the city of Venusport without warning. "Come on. Let's see what the professor has to say about this stuff."

They found the professor on the control deck bending over a microscope, studying samples taken from the flask. He peered intently into the eyepiece, wrote something on a pad, and then began searching through the pages of a reference book on chemicals of the solar system.

Lieutenant Claude stepped up to Hawks and saluted sharply. "Power deck reports they've got a clogged line, sir. It's in the gas exhaust."

Strong and Hawks looked at each other, and then Hawks turned to the young officer. "Send a couple of men outside to clear it."

"Aye, aye, sir," said Claude, and then hesitated. "Shall the men wear lead suits against possible radioactivity, sir?"

Before Hawks could answer, Newton turned to face the three men. The professor was smiling. "No need to take that precaution, Lieutenant. I never did tell you my third opinion, did I, Captain Strong?"

"Why, no, you didn't, sir," said Strong.

The professor held up a sheet of paper. "Here's your answer. Nothing but plain old Venusport topsoil. Pure dirt!"

"What?" exclaimed Hawks hastily, reaching for the paper.

"Well, blast me for a Martian mouse," muttered Strong under

his breath. "But how?"

Newton held up his hand. "Don't ask me how it got here. That isn't my line of work. All I know is that, without a doubt, the black cloud is nothing more than dirt. Plain ordinary dirt! And it comes from the area in and around Venusport. As a matter of fact, certain particles I analyzed lead me to believe it came from the exposition site!"

Hawks looked at Newton dumbfounded. "By the craters of Luna, man, we're a thousand miles over the exposition!"

The professor was stubborn. "I can't tell you how it got here, Commissioner Hawks. But I do know it's Venusian dirt. And that's final!"

Hawks stared at the elderly man for a second, still bewildered. Then he suddenly smiled and turned to Claude. "As soon as that exhaust is cleared, blast off for Venusport, Lieutenant. I'm going to find out who dirtied up the sky!"

*   *   *   *   *

Two hours later, when Captain Strong returned to his hotel in Venusport with Mike Hawks, he was surprised to see the three cadets of the *Polaris* crew slumped, sleepy-eyed, on a couch in the lobby.

"What are you doing here, boys?" he asked.

The three cadets came to attention and were wide awake immediately. Tom quickly related their suspicions of Wallace and Simms.

"And we've watched them every night, sir," Tom concluded. "I don't know what it is, but something certainly is going on in that shack they use for an office."

"Yes, sir," agreed Astro, "and no one is going to fool me about a rocket ship. I know when they blast off loaded and return light."

Strong turned to Hawks who said quietly, "Wallace and Simms are the only ones in this whole area that blast off regularly without a customs search."

"You mean," stammered Strong, "Wallace and Simms are dumping"—he could hardly say the word—"*dirt* in space?"

"They have a ship. The cadets say the ship blasts off loaded and returns light. And we've got the sky full of dirt. Venusian dirt!"

"But why?"

"I suggest we go out to the exposition grounds right now and ask them!" said Hawks coldly. "And believe me, they'd better have some rocket-blasting good answers!"

Carey Rockwell

CHAPTER 5

The great educational exhibits had long been closed and only a few sections of the amusement park of the big exposition remained open. The giant solar beacon, its brilliant colors changing every second, maintained a solemn solitary watch over the exhibition buildings, while here and there groups of fair visitors wandered wearily back to their hotels.

There was a sudden flurry of activity at the space-ride concession. Gus Wallace and Luther Simms tumbled out of the shack and raced into their ship. Once inside the ancient craft, they secured the hatch and turned toward each other smiling broadly. Wallace stuck out his hand.

"Put 'er there, Simms. We did it!"

The two men shook hands heartily.

"By the craters of Luna," said Simms, "I thought we'd never make it! And if we did, that it wouldn't be there!"

"But it was, Simms! It was! And now we've got it!"

"Yeah," agreed the other. "I never worked so hard in all my life. But it's worth it. Are we going to set the Solar Guard back on its ear!"

Wallace laughed. "Not only that, but think of what the boss will say when we show up with it!"

"You know, Wallace," said Simms, a sly look on his face, "we could take it and use it ourselves—"

"Don't even think a thing like that!" snapped Wallace.

"Oh, of course not," said Simms hurriedly. "It doesn't pay to cross the boss. There's enough here for all of us."

"You know," mused Wallace, "there's only one thing I regret."

"What's that?" asked his partner.

"That I didn't get a chance to kick the space dust out of that punk, Cadet Manning!"

"Forget him," said Simms, waving his hand. "You'll meet him again someday. Besides, why think about him, when you've got the whole universe at your finger tips?"

"You're right. But someday I'm going to catch him and tear him apart!" snarled Wallace. "Come on. We've got to change over to atomic drive on this baby. I don't want to hang around here any longer than I have to."

"Yeah," said Simms. "Be pretty stupid if we're caught now!"

The two men climbed down into the power deck and began the job of refitting the freighter from chemical to atomic drive. Having already outfitted the vessel with atomic engines, it was a simple matter to change the exhaust, reset the feed lines, and emplace the protective lead baffles. In an hour the two spacemen were ready to blast off.

"There she is," said Simms, standing back to survey their work. "As fast as anything in space, except the Solar Guard cruisers on hyperdrive."

"O.K.," said Wallace. "Let's get out of here!"

Minutes later, in a jet car speeding along the main highway toward the exposition grounds, Captain Strong, Mike Hawks, and the three cadets of the *Polaris* saw a rocket ship blast off. They watched it disappear into the dark space above.

"That might be they," said Strong to Hawks. "I'd better alert the patrol ship near the space station and tell them to pick them up."

"That couldn't be Wallace and Simms, sir," said Astro.

"How do you know, Astro?" asked Strong.

"That was an atomic-powered ship. The wagon Wallace and Simms have is a chemical job. I know the sound of her jets almost as well as I do the *Polaris*."

Hawks looked at Strong.

"You can depend on Astro's opinion, Mike," said Strong. "He was born with a rocket wrench in his hand and cut his teeth on a reactor valve."

They soon reached the outskirts of the exposition grounds and were forced to slow down as they wound their way through the darkened streets. In the amusement section, the last of the whirlaway rides and games of chance had closed down and only the occasional roar of a caged animal in the interplanetary zoo disturbed the night.

Hawks drove the low, sleek jet car around the fair, taking a short cut through the outdoor mercuryball field and pulled up in front of the *Polaris*.

The five spacemen turned toward the concession site across the promenade and stopped, aghast.

"Gone!" exclaimed Strong. "Astro, you made a mistake! It was their ship we saw blasting off. It's too late to warn the space-station patrol. Wallace and Simms could be anywhere in space now!"

"But, sir," protested Astro, "I'm certain that an atomic-powered ship blasted off. And their old freighter was a chemical burner!"

"Well," said Hawks resignedly, "they're not here."

"Come on," said Strong, getting out of the jet car. "Let's take a look around."

Strong and Hawks hurried across the street to the empty lot and the three cadets followed.

"Take it easy, Astro," said Tom, when he saw the big Venusian gripping his fists in frustration. "Anyone could make a mistake."

"That's just it," said Astro. "I'm not mistaken! Those jokers must have changed over from chemical fuel to reactant drive!"

"But why?" asked Roger. "That would cost more than they could make in ten years of hauling passengers on joy rides!"

Astro whirled around and faced the two cadets. "I'm telling

you the ship that blasted off from here was an atomic drive. I don't know any more than that, but I *do* know that!"

There was a sudden shout from Strong and the three boys hurried to the shack. The Solar Guard captain and the exposition commissioner were standing inside and playing the beam of an electric torch around the walls.

"Looks as though you were right about the atomic drive, Astro," said Strong. He flashed the light into one corner where a tangled jumble of lines lay on the floor. "That's feed-line gear for a chemical burner, and over there"—he played the light on some empty cartons—"is what's left of the crate's lead baffling it shipped in. They must have changed over to atomic drive recently."

Astro accepted the statement with a nod. It wasn't in the nature of the big cadet to boast. Now that the secret of the ship had been resolved, he turned, like the others, to the question of why?

"I think the best thing we can do," said Strong, "is to spread out and search the whole area. Might find something to indicate where they went." Commissioner Hawks nodded his head in agreement.

While Tom, Roger, and Astro searched outside, Strong and Hawks went through the drawers of the dusty desk standing in one corner.

"Nothing here but a record of the flights they made, bills for chemical fuel delivered, and the like," said Hawks at last. "They were losing money on the operation, too. Think they might have just gotten fed up and pulled out?"

Strong was rummaging around in one corner of the shack.

"I'd go along with that, but for one thing, Mike," he said. "Take a look at this." He held up a small cloth bag. "There's dirt in the bottom of this bag. And there are about fifty more bags in that corner."

"Dirt!" exclaimed the commissioner.

"Yep," said Strong grimly. "So we found out who was dumping the dirt. But we still haven't found out why."

"Or where it came from," said Hawks.

Strong tossed the bag into the corner. "Well, I guess I'd better make a report to Commander Walters."

Hawks moved to the corner where the pile of chemical feed-line equipment lay on the floor. "Want to take a look at this stuff? Might be something important in it."

Strong thought a moment. "We can have the cadets do that. I want to get this report off to Walters right away, and issue an order to pick up Wallace and Simms."

"On what charges, Steve?" asked the commissioner. "I mean, what's wrong with what they've done?" The commissioner's question was based on one of the cardinal rules among all Solar Guard officers of authority. "Has the man committed any crime?"

Steve realized this and answered slowly. "They've changed over to reactor drive without a license or permission. That's a violation of the space code, section twenty-one, paragraph A. That is punishable by a suspension of space papers, and if the intention proved to be willful neglect of the code, a year on a penal asteroid. I think we can get them on that."

The captain stepped to the door and called the cadets.

"Find anything?" he asked, when they entered the shack.

"Nothing, sir," replied Tom. "Except more evidence that they changed over to atomic drive."

"That's enough" said Strong. "I'm going to send a report to Commander Walters. Is the teleceiver on the *Polaris* hooked up, Roger?"

"Yes, sir," replied Roger. "But Astro will have to start up the auxiliary generators to give you power."

"Very well, then," said Strong. "Corbett, you give Astro a hand on the power deck. And while we're gone, Manning, you go through that feed-line junk there in the corner and see if there's anything important in it!"

"Aye, aye, sir," replied Roger.

Strong and Hawks, followed by Tom and Astro, left the shack and hurried to the *Polaris*.

On the power deck, Tom and Astro made the necessary connections on the generator, and in a few minutes, as power surged through the ship, Strong flipped on the teleceiver.

"Attention! Attention! This is Captain Strong on the *Polaris* calling Commander Walters at Space Academy! Earth emergency circuit, priority B—"

In a few moments the Solar Guard officer's call had been picked up by a monitor station on Earth and relayed directly to Space Academy. Commander Walters was roused out of bed, and when he appeared on the teleceiver screen, Strong saw he was still in sleeping dress.

"Sorry to disturb you, sir," said Strong, "but something has come up here at the exposition that needs your immediate attention."

"That's quite all right, Steve," said the commander with a smile. "What is it? Manning get into more trouble?"

"No, sir," answered Strong grimly. "I wish it were as simple as that." He quickly related the details of the strange dirt cloud and his suspicions of Wallace and Simms. Walters' expression grew serious.

"I'll get out an emergency bulletin on them at once, Steve. Meantime, you have full authority to head an investigation. Use any service you need. I'll confirm my verbal order with official orders at once. Get on this thing, Steve. It sounds serious."

"I will, sir, and thanks!" said Strong.

"End transmission!"

"End transmission," returned Strong, flipping off the teleceiver and turning to the ship's intercom. "Attention, power deck! Corbett, you and Astro go back to the shack and give Roger a hand. I'm going to work with the commissioner here setting up search operations."

"Aye, aye, sir," replied Tom from the power deck.

The two cadets hurriedly closed the power units and left the ship.

"Did you hear what Captain Strong said, Astro?" asked Tom.

"Search operations."

"I wonder what's up," the big Venusian remarked. "They don't set up search operations unless it's awfully serious!"

"Come on," urged Tom. "Maybe Roger's found something."

They entered the shack together and Tom called out, "Say, Roger, Captain Strong just spoke to Commander Walters at the Academy and—"

The curly-haired cadet stopped short. "Astro, look!"

"By the rings of Saturn!" exclaimed the big cadet.

The two cadets stood gaping at a huge hole in the middle of the room. The wooden floor was splintered around the edges of the opening and several pieces of the chemical feed-line equipment lay close to the edge, with trailing lines leading down into the hole. They heard a low moan and rushed up to the hole, flashing their lights down into it.

"Great galaxy!" yelled Tom. "Astro, look! It's a shaft! It must be a thousand feet deep!"

"And look!" bellowed Astro. "There's Roger! See him? He's hanging there! His foot's caught in that feed-line cable!"

The big cadet leaned over the hole and shouted, "Roger! Roger! Are you all right?"

There was no answer from the shaft. Nothing but the echo of Astro's voice.

CHAPTER 6

"Easy, Astro," said Strong, standing behind the big cadet. "Pull that line up slowly and gently."

"Yes, sir," gasped Astro. He didn't have to be told to pull the rope with caution. He knew only too well that the slightest jar or bump against the side of the shaft might dislodge Roger's unconscious body from the tangle of line, causing him to fall to the bottom of the shaft. How far down the shaft went, none of the anxious spacemen around the hole in the splintered floor knew. And they didn't want to use Roger's body to find out!

"I'll give you a hand, Astro," said Commissioner Hawks. He reached for the line, but the big cadet warned him away.

"That's all right, sir," he said. "He's almost up now."

Astro pulled gently, hand over hand, until Roger's limp body was a mere foot from the edge.

"Grab him, quick!" he panted.

Immediately Strong and Hawks were down on their knees at the edge of the hole. Each taking an arm, they pulled Roger out and laid him gently on the floor of the shack. They

Carey Rockwell

crouched over him and began a quick examination.

"How is he, sir?" asked Tom, hovering anxiously over the still form of his friend. "Will he be all right?"

Strong didn't answer for a moment, continuing his hurried, though careful check. Then he sat back on his heels and sighed in relief. "A few bruises but no broken bones, thank the universe. He's just suffering from shock. A day or so in sick bay and he'll be good as new."

"I'll take him over there right away, Steve," offered Hawks.

"Thanks, Mike," replied Strong. Then as he and the commissioner lifted the still form of the cadet and started to carry him out of the shack, he turned to Astro. "Blast over to the *Polaris* and call Solar Guard headquarters in Venusport. Tell them to send an emergency crew down here right away."

"Aye, aye, sir," snapped the big Venusian and dashed out of the shack.

Turning back to Hawks, Strong said, "Corbett and I will stay here and try to find out where that shaft leads."

"All right, Steve," nodded the commissioner. "Too bad we had to find out where that dirt came from the hard way."

Reaching the jet car, the two men placed Roger in the back seat, and Hawks slid in under the wheel to start the powerful jets. Just then Astro, racing back from the *Polaris*, pulled up breathlessly.

"Solar Guard crew is on the way, sir," he reported. He glanced anxiously into the back seat of the jet car.

"All right, Astro," said Strong gently, "take care of Roger." Strong gestured to the back seat and without a word Astro leaped in beside his friend. Hawks stepped on the accelerator and the car shot away in a roar of blasting jets.

Tom and Captain Strong watched the car disappear and then turned back to the shack. Each felt the same emotion, an unspoken determination to see that Wallace and Simms paid dearly for causing the accident.

Re-entering the shack, they began a careful examination of the shaft. Strong played his emergency light down the sides, but the beam penetrated only a short distance.

"We'll leave a note for the emergency crew," said Strong. "Our belt communicators might not work so far underground."

"You're going down, sir?" asked Tom.

Strong nodded. "If necessary. Tie that valve on the end of the rope Astro used and lower it into the shaft. If we can touch bottom with it, we'll climb down and see what Wallace and Simms were after."

"Yes, sir," said Tom. He took the length of rope, tied the heavy metal valve to the end, and began lowering it into the shaft. Strong continued to play the light down the shaft until the valve disappeared into the darkness.

"Rope's getting short, sir," warned Tom. "Only have about two hundred feet left."

Strong glanced at the remaining coils of line on the floor. "I'll get more from the *Polaris*, if we need it," he said. "How long was that line to begin with?"

"It's a regulation space line, sir," said Tom. "Astro took it out of the emergency locker. It's about twelve hundred feet."

By this time the line, hanging straight down the shaft, had become increasingly heavy. Suddenly it grew slack.

"I think I've hit bottom, sir," cried the cadet. "But I can't pull the valve back up again to make sure."

Strong grabbed the end of the line and helped the cadet pull it back up a short distance. Then they dropped the line again and felt a distinct slackening of weight.

"That's bottom all right," said Strong. "Take this end of the line, run it out of the window on your right, and back through the one on your left. Then make it fast."

"Yes, sir," said Tom. He jumped out of the window, trailing the rope after him, and reappeared almost immediately through the other window to tie a loop in the line. After checking the knot and testing the line by throwing his full weight against it, Strong stripped off his jacket and wrapped it about the line to prevent rope burns. Then, hooking the emergency light on his belt, he stepped off into the shaft. Tom watched his skipper lower himself until nothing but the light, a wavering pin point in the dark hole, could be seen. At last the light stopped moving and Tom knew Strong had reached the bottom.

"Halloooooooo!" The captain's voice echoed faintly up the dark shaft. "The belt communicators don't work!" he yelled. "Come on down!"

"Be right with you, sir!" yelled Tom. He scratched a message on the wooden floor of the shack for the emergency crew. Then he stripped off his jacket, wrapped it around the rope, secured the light to his belt, and stepped off into the darkness.

Slowly, his hands tight around the rope through his jacket, Tom slipped down the deep shaft. He kept his eyes averted from the black hole beneath him, looking instead at the sides of the shaft. Once, when he thought he had gone about seven hundred feet, he saw that he was passing through a stratum of thick clay and could see the preserved bones of long-dead mammals, protruding from the side of the shaft.

Finally Tom's feet touched solid ground and he released the rope. It was cold in the bottom of the shaft and he hastily put his jacket back on.

"Captain Strong?" he called. There was no answer. Tom flashed the light around and saw a low, narrow tunnel leading off to his left.

He walked slowly, and the newly dug sides of the tunnel seemed to close in on him menacingly. It was quiet. Not the blank silence of space that Tom was used to, but the deathlike stillness of a tomb. It sent chills up and down his spine. Finally he stepped around a sharp bend and stopped abruptly.

"Captain Strong!"

The Solar Guard officer was stooping over, his light resting on the ground, reading something he held in his hand. He looked up at Tom and jerked his thumb back over his shoulder. Tom flashed his light in that direction.

"By the rings of Saturn!" exclaimed Tom. There in front of him, ripped open like a can of sardines, was the gleaming metal skin of the time capsule! The dirt floor of the tunnel

Carey Rockwell

around Strong and beside the capsule was littered with audio spools, sound disks, micropapers, and stereo slides.

Tom kneeled down beside his skipper and stammered, "What—what does it mean, sir?"

"It means," answered Strong slowly, "that we're dealing with two of the cleverest men in the universe! If they've stolen what I think they have, the entire Solar Guard, Solar Alliance, and just about everyone in the universe is at their mercy!"

*　*　*　*　*

"How do you feel, Roger?" asked Astro.

The blond-haired cadet sat up in bed, dangled his feet over the side, and rubbed his neck. He groaned as he moved. "I don't think I'm going to dance much this month, if that answers your question. I feel like every bone in my body was broken!"

"They very nearly were, Cadet Manning," said the medical officer, standing near by.

"What happened, Manning?" asked Commissioner Hawks.

"I really don't know, sir," replied Roger. "I was moving the junk out of the corner of the shack so I could examine it. I was piling it up in the middle of the floor when—wham—something gave way and I took a header into nowhere!" He looked at Astro. "Now suppose *you* tell me what happened!"

Astro told Roger about finding him dangling at the end of the tangled feed lines. Then he said, "Tom and Captain Strong are out there now, waiting for one of the Solar Guard emergency crews."

"Well, what are we hanging around here for?" asked Roger, and hopped off the bed. He groaned, staggered, and then straightened up. "Nothing to worry about," he said, as Astro rushed to his side. "I'm as good as new!"

"What do you say, Doctor?" asked Hawks.

The doctor hesitated a moment and then smiled. "Well, Commissioner, Cadet Manning has several strained muscles in his back, but the best treatment for that is exercise."

Hawks nodded and signed a release slip which the doctor gave him. Astro helped Roger put on his space boots, and five minutes later they were speeding back to the exposition grounds in the commissioner's jet car. As they sped through the streets, the two cadets speculated on what they would find at the bottom of the shaft. Arriving at the shack, they were immediately challenged by an enlisted Solar Guardsman.

"Halt!" said the guard gruffly. "Advance slowly for recognition!"

With Commissioner Hawks leading the way, Roger and Astro walked up to the guard.

"Say," said Roger, nudging Astro, "look at what's going on around here!"

"Yeah," agreed Astro, wide-eyed. "Something must be plenty hot to have guards posted!"

Hawks was immediately recognized by the guard, but he still stubbornly demanded proof of their identity. Hawks, Roger, and Astro hauled out their Solar Guard identification disks, small metal plates with their images engraved in the shiny metal. On the other side was a detailed description of the bearer.

"Very well, sir," said the guard and let them pass.

In the pale light of dawn, feverish activity could be seen taking place around the shack. Two huge jet vans, filled with every possible piece of emergency equipment, were parked near by. The *Polaris* had been taken over as a temporary headquarters and the area was crowded with scarlet-clad enlisted men. Astro could hear the hum of generators on the *Polaris* and immediately felt concern for his power deck.

Proceeding to the shack they were again challenged by a guard and again had to produce their identification disks before entering. Once inside, they were amazed at the transformation. An aluminum tripod, ten feet tall, had been erected over the hole in the floor, and several steel cables, connected to a motor-driven steel drum, were looped over the apex of the tripod, one hanging straight down into the shaft. A thick plastic hose hung over the edge of the shaft, jerking spasmodically as air was pumped into the dark hole.

"By the craters of Luna," cried Hawks, "what's going on here?"

A young lieutenant stepped up to the commissioner and saluted sharply. "Lieutenant Silvers, sir. Second-in-command to Captain Allison of the emergency crew."

Hawks returned the salute and Lieutenant Silvers continued.

"Captain Strong, Cadet Corbett, and Captain Allison are at the bottom of the shaft, sir. The cage will be up in a moment and you may go down if you care to."

"Thank you, Lieutenant," said Hawks.

"Congratulations, Cadet Manning," said Silvers. "I understand you had a close call in the shaft."

"I did, sir," said Roger. "It was *very* close."

A light suddenly flashed on and the four spacemen turned to watch a large wire cage rise out of the shaft. It was built in three sections, each seven feet high. A ladder on one side of the cage gave easy access to the higher and lower levels. Astro climbed to the top section while Hawks took the lower. Roger stepped into the center section to avoid a climb. An enlisted man secured the gates and turned on the motor. The cage dropped through the shaft with sickening speed.

A minute later it began to brake slowly, finally coming to a dead stop at the bottom of the shaft. They were met by a Solar Guardsman who directed them into the tunnel, now illuminated by a row of flowing, self-powered emergency lights. Silently, but with rising excitement, the two cadets followed Hawks through the brightly lighted shaft, a thousand feet below the surface of the planet.

Turning the last corner in the tunnel they came upon Strong, Tom, and Captain Allison huddled near the torn side of the time capsule. They could hear Strong talking to Tom.

"There is a vault on every spaceship in the Solar Alliance, Tom," Strong was explaining. "The vault is locked before blast-off and opened after landing by a light-key operated only by a trusted spaceport security officer. This key flashes a series of light vibrations, in sequence, into the electromagnetic lock on the vault. It's really nothing more than a highly developed flashlight except that it flashes multiple combinations of lights, each containing certain electronic vibrations. The electromagnetic lock can only be opened with the proper combinations of colors and vibrations flashed by the light-key. Of course each ship has a different code of colors and vibrations, but the code itself wouldn't be hard to crack. The big thing would be to have an adjustable light-key, so that if one combination of colors and light vibrations do not work, you can try another. In that way you could open any energy lock on any vault in the system."

"And Wallace and Simms—" Tom hesitated.

"Yes, Corbett," said Strong grimly. "Wallace and Simms stole an information sound spool from the capsule. On that spool was a detailed description of the energy lock and the adjustable light-key. There were only seven keys in the system up to now. If we don't catch Wallace and Simms, there'll be eight."

"Great galaxy," Commissioner Hawks broke in. "This will ruin the exposition! The Alliance will close it after—"

Strong waved a calming hand at Hawks. "I've already spoken to Commander Walters at Space Academy, Mike," he said. "He wants this to remain a secret. No one knows about it besides us, and no one will. I'm taking your oaths, your spaceman's word, that it will remain a secret. There's no use in starting a panic. You'll keep the exposition going as if nothing had happened."

"But what can the Solar Guard do, sir?" asked Tom.

"We'll start the greatest search the system has ever seen," replied Strong calmly. "But the order for their arrest will be issued for some other violation." The Solar Guard officer suddenly noticed Roger for the first time.

"Oh, Manning!" he said, smiling. "Good to see you. How do you feel?"

"O.K., sir," replied Roger. "But I'd feel a lot better if those space crawlers didn't have the combination to every safe and vault in the universe!"

Strong nodded. "This is one of the cleverest crimes in history. And in searching for Wallace and Simms, we'll have to be twice as smart as they are!"

"Yes, sir," said Tom. "First we have to figure out what they will do, and then figure out how we're going to beat them!"

"That's right, Tom," nodded Strong. "And by the stars, if we don't beat them, the only safe place left for the credits and securities of the people in the system will be behind rows of paralo-ray guns!"

CHAPTER 7

"Attention! Attention! This is Captain Maitland of the rocket cruiser *Orion* reporting to Captain Strong at Space Academy. Come in, Strong!"

High in the Tower of Galileo overlooking Space Academy, the Solar Guard officer, his face showing the strain of the last three-weeks' futile search for Wallace and Simms, flipped on the teleceiver and replied, "Strong here. Go ahead, Maitland."

Tom, Astro, Roger, and Commander Walters stood behind Strong and waited tensely for the last report to come in. Mainland's voice crackled through millions of miles of space.

"We've searched space quadrants A through D, sections twenty-one through one hundred thirty-eight. Constant six-way radar sweep of the area. No sign of Wallace and Simms."

Strong sighed deeply and replied, "All right, Maitland. Thank you. You may return to base. End transmission."

"End transmission!" signaled Maitland, and the crackling static died out in the quiet room.

Walters stepped forward and placed his hand on Strong's shoulder. "Don't let it get you down, Steve," he said. "I saw the zone search you set up for those two. No one could have done more."

"Maybe not, sir," said Strong, getting up, "but we didn't catch them."

"Not yet," frowned the commander grimly, "but we will! Well, there's nothing else to do here. That was the last patrol ship to report, so you might as well close up shop."

He turned to the cadets, who had been reassigned from the exposition as aides to Captain Strong in his search for Wallace and Simms. "You three come with us," said Walters. "I've got an idea and I want all of you to hear it."

Strong and the boys followed the commander out of the Academy communications center down to his luxuriously furnished office.

"Perhaps," said Walters, settling back in his chair and lighting an enormous pipe filled with red Venusian tobacco, "perhaps we have been hunting the fox with the wrong kind of dogs."

"Assuming that Wallace and Simms are the foxes in this case and the Solar Guard the hunting dogs, what would you suggest, sir?" asked Strong.

Walters puffed several times and eyed Strong. "I was going to suggest that you and the cadets become merchant spacemen for a while and take a look at some of the uglier places of the Solar Alliance. Go right into the foxes' den dressed as foxes!"

"Ummmmh," mused Strong. "It is an idea."

"Give it a try, anyway," urged Walters. "Take that old freighter we confiscated from the Titan smugglers, the *Dog Star*. Wander around for a few weeks and see what you can pick up. We have the advantage, since only a few of us know *why* we're looking for Wallace and Simms. It might make finding them a little easier."

Strong looked at the cadets and then back at the commander. "It might just work, at that, sir," he said at last.

"Work your way around to Venusport," said Walters. "Let it be known that you four are—well, willing to do just about anything for a credit."

Strong and the cadets smiled. "All right, sir," said the young captain. "We'll start right away."

"No!" replied the commander firmly. "You'll start in the morning. Right now, I'm ordering you to hit the sack and get some rest. You're not going to catch those two with speed. You'll need brains and cleverness."

"Very well, sir," said Strong as he stood up. "And I want to thank you for giving us this assignment."

"No question about it," answered the commander. "If you have a tough job to do, you put your best team to work on it, and the job will get done!"

It was difficult for the three cadets, who had been standing to one side listening, to suppress a smile. They saluted and followed Strong from the room. He left them at the slidestairs with orders to be ready to blast off at 0800 hours.

Tom was silent as he climbed into his bed in the *Polaris* unit's quarters on the forty-second floor. Roger and Astro fell asleep almost as soon as their heads touched their air-foam pillows, but the curly-haired cadet lay with arms under his head, staring up at the ceiling. He felt uneasy about the task that faced them. He wasn't afraid for himself, or Roger, or Astro. Something he couldn't put his finger on bothered the young spaceman.

He reviewed Wallace and Simms' entire operation. He remembered the two men had struck him as not being too bright. Their success in stealing the secret of the adjustable light-key, and their methods, plus their complete disappearance, just didn't add up. He made up his mind to speak to Captain Strong about it in the morning. As soon as the matter was settled in his mind, he was asleep.

* * * * *

At exactly 0800 hours the three cadets and Captain Strong appeared at the Academy spaceport dressed in the severe black tight-fitting trousers and jacket of merchant spacemen. Quietly eluding all friends and acquaintances, they entered the confiscated freighter that had been prepared for space flight during the night and began acquainting themselves with the ship's equipment.

When Astro reported the power deck ready and Roger cleared their course, Tom called the traffic-control tower for blast-off clearance.

"Take it easy on the first hop," said Strong. "There's no hurry and I want to be sure we get this crate off in one piece." Smiling confidently at the control-deck cadet, he turned away to his quarters. He was aware of the effect that being left alone had on the cadets. He had learned early in his associations with Tom, Roger, and Astro that they bore responsibility well, and a challenge to do a good job would assure him the job would be done efficiently.

"Stand by to raise ship!" Tom's voice crackled confidently over the ship's intercom.

Strong sat on an acceleration cushion and strapped himself in. He heard Tom's voice counting off the seconds for blast-off.

"... Five—four—three—two—one—*zero*."

As the rockets burst into a loud roar, the freighter lurched from the ground and thundered up into the atmosphere, pushing Strong deep into his acceleration cushion. Minutes later, he felt the freedom of free-fall space. In a strange ship, the *Polaris* crew had begun a strange mission.

During the flight to Luna City, their first stop on the tour of the hangouts of outlawed spacemen across the solar system, Strong briefed his cadets on a plan of action.

"I think it'll be better if we split up into two teams. You work with me, Corbett, and Astro will team up with Manning. We'll operate like simple tramp spacers. Our space papers have new last names, but the same first names, so there won't be any slip-ups when we speak to each other. From now on, if we happen to meet, you'll all call me Steve and I'll call you by your first names. Is that clear?"

The cadets nodded.

"All right," continued Strong. "Now, when we arrive in a city, Tom and I will go to one section, while you two go to another. Visit the toughest-looking places you can find. Talk,

talk to anyone that wants to talk. Buy people drinks. Let it slip that you're not exactly on the right side of the space code. Then, if you feel you have a sympathetic listener, mention Wallace and Simms. Say you have heard of the trouble they're in. Say you know them, that you're old friends, and hint that you have something that they need very badly. Just keep talking and pulling for information. Got that?"

Again the three cadets nodded silently.

"Wear your paralo-ray guns at all times and keep your belt communicators hidden beneath your jackets," Strong warned. "If one team gets into a tight spot, call the other right away. But don't call unless it's absolutely necessary!" Strong paused and glanced at the tele-scanner. "We're getting close to Luna City. We'll touch down at the municipal spaceport and go through the regular routine of customs search just to establish ourselves as tramp spacemen."

"How long will we stay in each city, sir?" asked Tom.

"Watch that 'sir,' Tom," snapped Strong. "Might as well begin to forget it now."

"O.K., Steve," replied Tom sheepishly.

"To answer your question, we'll stay in each city only as long as there might be something to be gained by staying. We'll live aboard the *Dog Star*. But stay away from the ship as much as possible. If anyone questions you, tell them you're looking for cargo. But in case they take you up on it and offer you a cargo haul, you always want more money for the job."

Roger grinned. "That could be fun."

"Be clever, but be tough. Some of the people you'll run into are the most ruthless men in the universe. They are just the ones that might know something about Wallace and Simms."

Strong cautioned them against drinking rocket juice, suggesting they drink Martian water instead. The briefing was interrupted by the automatic warning beep from the tele-scanner informing them that they had passed the outer beacon on the approach to the municipal spaceport on the Moon. The four spacemen immediately began the routine task of landing their ship safely on the satellite colony.

An hour later, as gray-clad customs men finished searching the empty ship, Roger waited for final clearance at the air lock of the freighter. When the last of the men were leaving the ship, Roger stopped two of them.

"Say, ground hogs," drawled Roger, "where's the best place to get something to eat?"

The two men stopped and turned to face the cadet, their eyes cold and unfriendly. "Why don't you space drift blast out of here?" asked one of them.

"Yeah," agreed the other, "your kind aren't welcome in Luna City."

Roger shrugged his shoulders and turned away. The two customs officers continued down the gangway. "Those young punks," muttered one, "they get themselves a berth on a crummy freighter and think they're real hot space aces when they're nothing but wet fire-crackers!"

Strong had appeared at Roger's side and heard the last remark.

"What was that about, Roger?" he asked, nodding toward the disappearing customs men.

Roger smiled. "Just seeing if I could get by."

"They certainly gave us a good going over," said Strong grimly. "I think our disguise is perfect. Those fellows don't miss much."

"I heard them talking, Steve," said Roger. "They recognized the ship and know its reputation for smuggling."

"Yes," agreed Strong. "And your remark will make them sure to watch every move we make. But that's just what we want. News of that sort has a way of getting around. And anyone interested in a ship with a reputation for smuggling is someone we're interested in."

Astro walked up, and with a brief nod Roger followed the big cadet down the gangway. As they walked across the concrete surface of the spaceport, Tom appeared at Strong's elbow.

"I'm ready to go, Steve," he said. "The ship's secure."

"Very well, Tom," said Strong. "But from now on, keep your eyes and ears open. It only takes one slip to make a dead spaceman!"

CHAPTER 8

"See that fellow over there, Steve?" whispered Tom. "The one with the scar on his face?"

"Yeah," replied the disguised Solar Guard officer. "I've been watching him too. And I think he's had his eye on us."

Tom and Captain Strong were sitting in a small restaurant near the spaceport, drinking Martian water and discussing the shadowy characters that lounged around the stuffy little room.

"I'll walk over to the bar," said Strong. "Maybe he doesn't want to talk to two of us together. You go over and see if you can strike up a conversation."

"Good idea, sir—uh—Steve," said Tom.

Strong got up and with an exaggerated swagger walked to the small bar. From the mirror in back of the bar, he could see Tom rise and saunter over to the man who sat on the opposite side of the room.

For three days, Roger, Astro, Tom, and Strong had wandered through the bars, restaurants, and cheap hotels of Spaceman's Row in Luna City searching for information that would lead them to Wallace and Simms. Each night they returned to the freighter to exchange, sift, and analyze the bits of information gathered, but for three nights they had come up with a total of nothing. Finally, Strong had decided that this would be the last night they would spend in Luna City. It was after making this decision that he and Tom spotted the scar-faced man sitting alone in one corner.

Strong saw Tom stop at the table, say a few words, then sit down and order drinks. Tom and the scar-faced man continued their conversation, now leaning across the table talking in whispers, stopping only long enough for the waiter to serve the drinks. Strong noticed that the scar-faced man paid for them and smiled to himself. That was a step in the right direction. He obviously wanted something from Tom.

Suddenly the young cadet looked up and motioned for him to come over to the table. Strong merely lounged against the bar and nodded carelessly. Taking his time, he finished his glass of Martian water, then swaggered across the crowded room to the table.

Tom glanced up casually and then turned to his companion at the table. "This is my skipper," he said. "Name's Steve. You gotta job to do, Steve'll do it. Anything, anywhere, any time," he paused, and then added with a smirk, "for a *price*!"

The scar-faced man looked up at Steve. His eyes traced a pattern over the tall man, noting the broad shoulders, the piercing eyes, and the bulge of a paralo-ray gun in his jacket. He pushed a chair back with a foot and managed a smile in spite of the scar that twisted his features into an ugly mask. "Sit down, Steve. My name's Pete."

Strong accepted the invitation silently. At close range, he saw the man was more disfigured than he had noticed from the bar. The scar on his face reached from his left ear across his cheek and down to his neck. Pete saw him looking at the scar and smiled again. "Funny thing about scars. I got one, but I don't have to look at it. I just stay away from mirrors and I remember myself as I was before I got it. So look all you want. You're the one that's got to suffer for it."

Ignoring the man's bitter tone of voice, Strong growled, "I'm not interested in what you look like. You got something to haul; we got a ship to haul it. Name your cargo and destination, and we'll name a price."

"Ain't as simple as that," said Pete craftily. "I gotta know more about you before we talk business."

"What for instance?" asked Strong.

"For instance, who do you know on Spaceman's Row that can give you a reference?"

Tom spoke up quickly without looking at Strong. "Suppose I told you I helped pull a job a couple of weeks ago that was worth a hundred thousand credits?" He settled back, casually glancing at Strong and receiving an imperceptible nod in return.

"A hundred thousand, eh?" said Pete with interest. "Not bad, not bad. What kind of a job was it?"

"Me and two other guys held up the Credit Exchange at the Solar Exposition at Venusport."

"Oh?" Pete was becoming extremely curious. "You in on the job too, Steve?"

Before Strong could answer, Tom spoke quickly. "No, I

bought a half interest in Steve's ship with my share of the take." Strong could hardly keep from smiling, so easily was the young cadet's tale growing.

"Then who *was* in on this job with you?" persisted the scar-faced man. "You look pretty young to pull a big job like that."

Tom glanced around the room and then leaned over the table before whispering, "Gus Wallace and Luther Simms."

"What?" exclaimed Pete. "Gus Wallace? A guy about six feet tall and two hundred pounds? Has a heavy rough voice?"

"That's the one," said Tom.

Pete's arm shot across the table like a snake and he grabbed Tom by the jacket. "Where is he?" he asked through clenched teeth.

No sooner had Pete touched Tom than Strong had his paralo-ray gun leveled at the scar-faced man. "Take your hands off him," he said coldly, "or I'll freeze you right where you are!"

Pete relaxed his grip and settled back into his chair. He glared at Tom and then at Strong.

"All right," snapped Strong. "Now *you* talk!"

Pete didn't say anything. Strong inched closer to the scar-faced man menacingly. "I said *talk*! Why do you want to know where Gus Wallace is? Maybe you're Solar Guard, eh? Trying to play a little trick on us. How do I know you haven't got a squad of MP's outside waiting to pick us up?"

Pete began to shift nervously. "You got me all wrong, Steve.

Carey Rockwell

I ain't Solar Guard."

"Why do you want to know where Gus Wallace is, then?" Strong persisted.

Pete hesitated and had to be prodded with the paralo-ray gun again by Strong. "Talk!" hissed Strong.

"You see this scar?" asked Pete. "Well, two years ago, on Spaceman's Row in Marsopolis, Gus slashed me in a fight. I swore I'd do the same for him when I caught him, but he's been running from me ever since."

"Marsopolis, eh?" asked Strong. "Two years ago?"

"Yeah."

"I think you're lying! You're Solar Guard."

"Honest, Steve," whined Pete. "That's the only reason I want him. Ask anybody. It happened in the Spacelanes Bar on New Denver Avenue. I bet there are five guys here right now who heard about it!"

Strong got up, pushing the gun back in his belt.

"Come on, Tom. I don't like the way your friend Pete answers questions."

"Wait a minute!" Pete rose from his chair, protesting.

Strong whirled around and faced the scar-faced man. "If I were you, Pete," he muttered, "I'd sit still and not ask any more questions. It isn't healthy!"

Without another word Strong walked out of the dingy

restaurant. Tom shrugged his shoulders in a helpless gesture and followed, leaving Pete alone and worried.

Outside in the street, his face bathed in the garish light of the vapor street lights, Strong stopped to wipe his forehead.

"Whew!" he gasped. "We certainly bulled our way through that one!"

"I felt the same way," said Tom. "But at least we have something to go on. You think he was suspicious?"

"No, Tom. He was so scared when I accused him of being tied up with the Solar Guard it threw him completely off stride."

"Well? Where do we go from here?" asked Tom.

"Back to the ship," replied Strong. "And as soon as Astro and Roger show up, we blast off for Marsopolis. Our next target is a joint called the Spacelanes!"

*   *   *   *   *

Against a backdrop of shimmering stars that studded the velvet black emptiness of space, the freighter *Dog Star* rocketed toward the red planet of Mars carrying the four spacemen on the next step of their search. Relaxing from the three arduous days on the Moon and able to be themselves once more, Strong and the three cadets rested and discussed every detail of their stay in Luna City. It was finally decided that their only real chance of tracing Wallace and Simms lay in the Spacelanes Bar. As they approached Mars, Strong outlined their next move.

"We'll do the same thing as we did in Luna City," he said.

"Split up. Only this time, we'll all go to the same place, the Spacelanes. Tom and I will go in first and do most of the nosing around. Astro and Roger will drift in later and hang around, just in case there's trouble."

The three cadets nodded their understanding, and when Strong turned to the teleceiver to make his report to Commander Walters at Space Academy, they took their stations for touchdown at Marsopolis.

His face impassive on the teleceiver screen, Commander Walters listened to Strong's report, and when the Solar Guard officer finished, he grunted his satisfaction.

"Do you have any news on Wallace and Simms, sir?" asked Strong.

"Yes, but my news isn't as good as yours," frowned Walters. "They've already made use of their knowledge of the light-key. They held up a Solar Guard transport en route to Titan and emptied her armory. They took a couple of three-inch atomic blasters and a dozen paralo-ray guns and rifles. Opened the energy lock with their adjustable light-key as easily as if it had been a paper bag. It looks as though they're setting themselves up for a long siege."

"Do you have any idea where they might be hiding, sir?"

"Somewhere in the asteroid belt, I believe," replied the commander. "They headed for the belt after they held up the transport."

"Well, we'll do what we can from our end, sir," said Strong. "Since Mars is closer to the asteroid belt than any other planet, they might be using Marsopolis as a hangout. Or someone might have seen them recently."

"Use whatever plan you think best, Steve. I'm counting on you."

"Thank you, sir."

"Spaceman's luck! End transmission."

"End transmission," replied Strong and flipped off the screen.

Fifteen minutes later, the *Dog Star* settled on a blast-scorched ramp at the Marsopolis spaceport, and after a hasty review of their plans, the four spacemen left the ship. Strong had a brief argument with a customs officer over a personal search for small arms. They were forced to leave their paralo-ray guns on the ship. Disgruntled, as far as the customs agents were concerned, Strong was actually pleased with the success of their disguise as merchant spacemen.

Tom and Strong found the Spacelanes Bar in the roughest and darkest section of Marsopolis. It was large and almost empty. But Tom noted that it was just like many other such places he had been in in Luna City. The walls were scarred and dirty, the floor littered, and the tables and chairs looking as if they had been used in a hundred fights. Behind a bar that ran the length of one wall, a heavy-set man with beady black eyes watched their approach.

"What's your pleasure, spacemen?" asked the bartender in a gruff voice.

Strong hesitated a moment and decided to play all his cards at one turn. "We'll have a thousand credits worth of information."

The barman's eyes narrowed into black slits. "What kind of

information would bring that kind of a price?" he asked.

"Information about a man," said Strong.

"What man?" asked the barman. He dropped his hand out of sight behind the bar. Tom's eye caught the move and he wished the customs men hadn't taken away their paralo-ray guns.

Just at that moment he heard Roger's unmistakable laugh and turned to see the blond cadet, followed by Astro, enter, cross the room, and slap the bar for service.

"Let me take care of these two," muttered the bartender and walked down to the end of the bar. Facing Roger and Astro, he snarled, "What'll it be?"

"Coupla bottles of Martian water," drawled Roger.

"Get out of here," roared the bartender. "We don't sell kids' drinks in here."

"Two bottles of Martian water!" growled Astro and leaned over the bar threateningly. Strong and Tom watched the performance with amused eyes. Without a word, the barman opened the bottles of Martian water and gave them to Roger and Astro. He turned back to Strong.

"These young rocketheads think they're so blasted tough," he sneered, "and then drink kids' soda pop."

Strong looked at Roger and Astro. "That fellow on the right," indicating Astro's size, "looks like he could be a little more than a child, if he got mad."

The barman snorted and leaned over the bar. "What about

that thousand credits?" he asked.

"What about it?" countered Strong.

"That's a lot of money just for information," said the barman.

"It's my money," replied Strong coolly, "and my business!"

"What kind of information you interested in," asked the bartender.

"I told you, information about a man," said Strong. "Gus Wallace. Happen to know him?" Strong pulled a roll of crisp credit notes out of his jacket pocket. The barman looked at them greedily.

"Maybe. What'cha want with him?" he asked.

"He knifed a friend of ours in here two years ago."

"Yeah?" drawled the barman. "Who?"

"Pete," answered Strong, suddenly realizing he didn't know the scar-faced man's last name.

"Pete? Pete who?" asked the barman craftily.

"What are you trying to do?" snapped Tom suddenly. "Play space lawyer? You know Pete was knifed in here by Gus Wallace two years ago! Carved up good!" He made a slashing gesture from his ear to his throat, indicating the scar on Pete's face.

"So you want Wallace, eh?" mused the bartender.

"We want him a thousand credits' worth," said Strong.

"You didn't tell me for what, yet."

"None of your space-blasting business," roared Strong. "You want the thousand or not?"

The bartender couldn't keep his eyes off the crisp roll of credit notes Strong rippled under his nose and hesitated. "Well, to tell you the truth, I ain't seen him for a long time."

"Then do you know anyone who has?" asked Strong.

"Hard to tell," said the bartender huskily. "But I do know the guy who would know if anyone does."

"Who?" asked Tom.

"On Venusport's Spaceman's Row. There's a joint called the Cafe Cosmos. Go there and ask for a little guy named Shinny. Nicholas Shinny. If anyone knows about Wallace, he'll know."

Tom's heart almost stopped. Nicholas Shinny was a retired spaceman who had taken part in his last adventure to Alpha Centauri, and was a good friend of Strong's and the *Polaris* unit. Shinny had always operated on the edge of the space code. Nothing illegal, but as Shinny himself put it, 'just bending the code a little, not breaking it.'

Tom spoke up. "That's only worth a hundred credits," he said.

"Whaddya mean!" snapped the barman.

"How would Nick Shinny know Gus Wallace?" asked Strong.

"They prospected the asteroids together years ago."

Strong dropped a hundred-credit note on the bar and turned away without another word. Tom followed, and as they passed Roger and Astro, a knowing look passed between them, and Tom gestured for them to follow.

Having heard the conversation, Astro and Roger walked over to the bartender who was folding the credit note before putting it in his pocket.

"You sell your information pretty cheap, spaceman," snarled Roger. "Suppose those two were Solar Guardsmen in disguise?"

The bartender paused, then shook his head. "Couldn't be!" he said.

"Why not?" asked Roger.

"Because the Solar Guard has a guy salted away that knows exactly where Wallace is."

CHAPTER 9

"That's the story, sir," said Strong to Commander Walters, after the Solar Guard captain had related the information he had wormed out of the bartender at the Spacelanes Bar and the news Roger and Astro had brought.

"All right, Steve," nodded the commander. "I'll have the man picked up right away and psychographed. Meantime, you go on to Venus and see Nicholas Shinny."

"Very well, sir," said Strong. "End transmission!"

"End transmission," acknowledged Walters. Strong flipped the switch and the teleceiver screen darkened.

Fifteen minutes later, the *Dog Star* blasted off from Mars, heading for Venus.

During the trip back to the young planet that was rapidly growing into a major industrial center rivaling Earth, Strong received a report from Space Academy that the bartender had been picked up. His name was Joseph Price, and after questioning him under truth serum, Solar Guard security officers found the man's mind to be so filled with criminal plots and counter-plots, it would take several weeks for the psychograph analyst to learn the name of the man he claimed would know the whereabouts of Wallace. This was disappointing news for Strong, especially since the report included news of a second, third, and fourth strike by Wallace and Simms on spaceships near the asteroid belt.

Reaching the starting place of their adventure, Venusport and the Solar Exposition, Strong and the three cadets went immediately to a small suburban section of the great city and the home of Nicholas Shinny.

Shinny lived comfortably in a small house made of Titan crystal, enjoying himself during the day catching Venusian fatfish and watching the stereos at night. Once an enlisted spaceman, he had been retired with full pension and was living in ease and comfort. When Strong and the three cadets arrived at the elderly spaceman's house, they found him busy teaching a young Venusian wolfhound puppy how to retrieve.

"Well, blast my jets!" cried the old man. "If it ain't Tommy, Roger, and the big fella, Astro! And Captain Strong!"

"Hello, Nick!" said Strong with a smile. "You're a sight for space-blind eyes!"

"Heh-heh-heh," cackled Shinny, his merry eyes twinkling against his deep space tan. "It's mighty good to see you boys. Come on in the house. I got a mess of fatfish just pulled out of the stream and some of the most delicious biscuits you ever had in your life!"

"Well, thanks, Nick," hesitated the captain. "But we're in—"

"Can't be in too much of a hurry to eat," snapped the old man with a grin. "Anything you got to say is better said when you got a bellyful of Molly's cookin'."

"Molly!" cried Tom. "But, Mr. Shinny—"

"When—" gulped Astro, "when did you—"

"Hey! Hold on!" cried the old spaceman. "Just damp your tubes there, youngsters! You're way off course. Molly ain't nothing but an electronic cook I got installed in the kitchen. She cooks better'n any space-brained woman and she never opens her mouth to give me any sass!"

The four spacemen laughed at Shinny's obvious indignation.

"Now come on!" he growled. "Let's eat. I'm hungry!"

Refusing to allow them to get near Molly, Shinny began pushing food into slots, compartments, turning on switches and punching buttons. In the cozy living room, Strong relaxed while the three cadets played with the Venusian wolfhound. Finally Shinny announced dinner and they fell to with gusto. There wasn't much talk during the course of the meal. Strong and the boys felt that Shinny would let them know when he was ready.

Finally the meal was over. Shinny sprawled in his chair, lit his pipe, then looked at his guests, his eyes twinkling. "All right, me friends, I think you've held back long enough. Let's have it."

Strong immediately told the old spaceman the entire story, from Wallace and Simms' false concession at the exposition to the present.

"You see, Nick," he concluded, "with an adjustable light-key enabling them to open any lock in the solar system, nothing is safe. Personally, I think it's only because they haven't a larger or faster ship and aren't better armed that they haven't tried more daring piracy. They'll reach that point soon, though. They've already robbed four ships for arms alone."

"I'll do anything I can to help you, Captain," said Shinny. "What is it you want to know?"

"We suspect that Wallace has a secret hide-out in the asteroid belt," said Strong. "Since you once prospected the asteroids with him I thought you might know where the hide-out is."

Shinny grew reflective and knocked the ashes out of his pipe before he answered. "That was a long time ago, Captain. More'n ten years. And Gus Wallace was a real square spaceman then. He didn't turn bad until after we split up and he met that other feller."

"What other fellow?" asked Strong.

Skinny paused. There was a hard glint in his eyes. "Bull Coxine!" He spat the name out as though it had left a bad taste in his mouth.

"Coxine!" exclaimed Strong.

"You heard me," snorted Shinny. "Bull Coxine and Gus Wallace got together after me and Wallace lost our stake hunting for uranium pitchblende in the asteroids and split up. Next thing I heard, him and Coxine was mixed up in that business up on Ganymede when the Credit Exchange was held up."

Strong's face had turned the color of chalk. "Coxine!" he repeated under his breath.

Noticing Strong's reaction to Shinny's statement, Tom asked,

"Who is Coxine, Captain Strong?"

Strong was silent and Shinny turned to the cadets.

"When your skipper here was a young feller just starting out in the Solar Guard," the old man explained, "he was on a routine flight out to Titan and there was a mutiny. Coxine was the ringleader. The captain joined up with Coxine after they had put his skipper in the brig. When he had Coxine's confidence, he regained control of the ship and sent Coxine and the others to a prison asteroid. Coxine has hated the captain ever since and swore to get him."

"But how did he pull the holdup on Ganymede, then?" asked Roger.

"Coxine escaped from the prison asteroid in a jet boat, disguised as a guard," continued Shinny. "Only man ever to escape. He drifted around in the belt for a while and was picked up by a freighter going to Ganymede. The freighter had been out rocket-hopping among the asteroids, collecting the prospectors' small supplies of uranium and taking the stuff back to Ganymede for refining. Wallace happened to be dead-heading on the freighter. When they got to Ganymede, and Coxine saw all the money lying around at the Credit Exchange to pay off the prospectors, he convinced Wallace to go in with him and they robbed the Exchange. Coxine was caught red-handed, but Wallace got away. In fact, the Solar Guard didn't know Wallace had anything to do with it. So Coxine was taken back to the prison asteroid, and Wallace has been driftin' around the system ever since."

"But, Mr. Shinny," asked Astro, "if you knew Wallace was tied up with the robbery of the Credit Exchange, why didn't you tell the Solar Guard before now?"

"Sonny," sighed Shinny, "most of what I know is space dust and space gas. But even so, I don't think Commander Walters or Captain Strong, or even you boys, would think much of me if I went around like an old space crawler, blowin' my jets all over the place."

Strong had listened to Shinny fill in the background of Bull Coxine with a thoughtful look in his eyes. He remembered all too clearly the mutiny on the ship out to Titan. Coxine had been an enlisted Solar Guard petty officer aboard the ship. He had made great strides in two years and was being considered as an officer candidate on the very day he tried to take over the ship. When Strong regained control later, he talked to Coxine, trying to find out why he had started the mutiny. But the man had only cursed him, swearing vengeance. Strong hadn't seen him since.

"So you think he would know where Wallace and Simms might be hiding out?" Strong asked finally.

"If anyone does," replied Shinny, "he does. And I'll tell you this, Captain, if you go to talk to him and I figger you will, you'll find him a lot tougher."

"Will I?"

"Well, take yourself, for instance. No reflection on you, of course, but take yourself. You're smart, you're hard, and you got a good mind. You're one of the best spacemen in the deep. Take all that and turn it bad. Real bad. Sour it with too many years on a prison asteroid and you've got a fire-eating rocket buster as tough and as rough as God and society can make him!"

The three cadets gulped and looked at Strong. They saw their skipper clench his teeth and ball his fists into tight knots.

"I know," said Strong in a hoarse whisper, "but if he knows where Wallace and Simms are, he'll tell me. You can bet your last credit, he'll tell me!"

Shinny paused reflectively. "I won't bet," he said simply.

*   *   *   *   *

The air inside the space shack was stale because of a faulty filter in the oxygen circulator that neither Wallace nor Simms bothered to clean. The two men lazed around in stocking feet and undershirts, listening to popular music coming over the audio receiver on a late pickup from one of the small Jovian satellite colonies near by.

"Pour me another cup of coffee, Simms," grunted Wallace.

The smaller man poured a cup of steaming black liquid and silently handed it over to his companion. They both listened as the music faded to an end and the voice of the announcer crackled over the loud-speaker.

"This audiocast has been beamed to space quadrants D through K, as a courtesy to the army of uranium prospectors working the asteroid belt. Hope you've enjoyed it, spacemen, and happy hunting!"

Wallace reached over and snapped off the receiver. "Thanks, pal." He laughed. "The hunting's been real good! We've got a full catch!" The giant spaceman laughed again.

"Yeah," agreed Simms. "I just went over the take. We've got enough money in that locker"—he indicated a black box on the floor—"to sit back and take it easy for the rest of our lives."

"Yeah?" snarled Wallace. "You mean sitting in the sun on a crummy lakeside, watching the birds and bees?"

"Gus," asked Simms thoughtfully, "you got any idea how much fun we can buy with the credits in that box?"

"Yeah, I have!" sneered Wallace, "and I know what a thousand times that much will buy too!"

Suddenly Simms turned and looked his partner in the eye. "What do you say we quit now, Gus? I mean it. We got plenty."

"You sound like you been exposed to too many cosmic rays!" said Wallace, tapping his head with one finger. "We've got the biggest secret in the system, the adjustable light-key plus an airtight hide-out, and you want to quit!"

"It ain't that," whined Simms. "It's the other deal. I don't mind going out and blasting a few freighters, but to try to—"

"Lissen," interrupted Wallace, "I'd rather try it and take the licking if we mess it up, than not try it and take that licking. I know which side of the space lane I'd better be on when the time comes!"

Simms hesitated and then sighed, "Yeah, I guess you're right."

"Come on. Let's listen to that story spool again."

"Oh, no," moaned Simms. "I know that spool by heart! We've heard it at least fifty times!"

"One slip-up," said Wallace, sticking his finger in Simms' face, "just one slip-up and we're finished! We've got to be sure!"

With a reluctant shrug of his shoulders, Simms poured another cup of coffee and sat on the side of his bunk while Wallace inserted the story spool in the audio playback.

They settled themselves and listened as a deep voice began to speak in a loud whisper.

"... The operation will take place on the night of October twenty-ninth at exactly twenty-one hundred hours. You will make your approach from section eleven, M quadrant—"

Simms jumped up abruptly and switched off the playback. Turning to Wallace, he pleaded, "I can't listen to it again! I know it by heart. Instructions on how to get to the time capsule; instructions on what to take, and how to build an adjustable light-key after we get the plans; instructions on how to hijack the first ship and what to take. Orders, information, instructions! I'm sick of listening. If you want to, go ahead, but I'm going to work on the ship!"

"O.K., O.K.," said Wallace, getting up. "Don't blow your jets. I hate the thing as much as you do. Wait a minute and I'll go with you."

The two men began climbing into space suits. In a few minutes they were dressed in black plastic suits with small round clear plastic helmets. They stepped into the air lock on one side of the room and closed a heavy door. Wallace adjusted the valve in the chamber and watched the needle drop until it showed zero.

"O.K.," said Wallace over his helmet spacephones. "All the air's out. Open the outer lock."

Simms cranked the heavy handle, and the door in the opposite wall of the chamber slowly swung open. They stepped out into the airless black void of space and onto the surface of an asteroid, drifting in the thickest part of the belt. Surrounding the asteroid were countless smaller secondary satellites circling the mother body like a wide curving blanket. The mother body was perfectly hidden from outside observation. It made a perfect base of operations for the two space pirates.

The freighter that they had used at the concession at the Solar Exposition and later to make their escape was a far different ship from the one now resting on the asteroid. Two powerful three-inch atomic blasters could be seen sticking out of the forward part of the ship. And near the stern, two gaping holes showed the emplacements for two additional guns not yet installed.

The two men walked over to the ship, and while Wallace entered the ship, Simms picked up a cutting torch and ignited it, preparing to finish the two holes in the stern.

When Wallace reappeared, he was carrying a coil of wire with a double plug to attach to the spacephones inside their helmets. He jammed the plug into Simms' helmet and then into his own. Simms' eyes lit up with surprise as he heard....

"...This is a general emergency announcement from Solar Guard headquarters. Squadrons A and B of the Marsopolis garrison will proceed to space quadrants W, sections forty-one to fifty. It is believed that Gus Wallace and Luther Simms are in that vicinity. Approach with caution, they are armed with atomic blasters and are believed to be psychologically unable to surrender. It is believed they will resist arrest...."

Carey Rockwell

The voice repeated the announcement and added a general call for the men, if they were listening, to surrender. Wallace pulled out the two plugs and grinned at Simms.

"Picked it up on the teleceiver inside the ship. Thought you might like to know how safe we are here."

Simms grinned back, "And how far off the track they are. Where is that space quadrant they think we're in?"

"Out past Saturn," said Wallace with a grin. "With the Mars garrison chasing us at one end of the system, we'll hit them on the other and be gone before they know what happened!"

Simms patted the barrel of the nearest atomic blaster. "And, spaceman, we're going to hit them hard!"

CHAPTER 10

"Stop your ship and be recognized!"

The rasping voice on the audioceiver was sharp. A command to be obeyed.

Tom turned away from the control board and looked at Strong who was already reaching for the ship's intercom.

"Full braking rocket thrust, Astro," he yelled into the microphone, "and make it quick or we'll all be blasted into protons!"

Tom and the captain gripped their chairs tightly as the ship bucked against the deceleration force of the powerful braking rockets. Gradually the freighter *Dog Star* slowed and came to a dead stop in space.

"Hey!" yelled Astro over the intercom from the power deck. "What's going on up there?"

"We've just entered the outer circle of defense on the prison asteroid, Astro," replied Strong. "We have to stop so they can sweep us with their radar and identify the ship."

"But I sent them a message in Solar Guard code that we were

coming," interjected Roger who was listening from the radar bridge.

"They still have to make sure it's us," said Strong.

"Identify yourselves!" commanded the voice over the audioceiver again.

"This is space freighter *Dog Star* under temporary command of Captain Strong of the Solar Guard," answered Strong.

"What's your business here?" demanded the voice again.

"Interrogation of one of your prisoners. We have sent a coded message, under code Z for Zebra to your prison commandant, Major Alan Savage. If you'll check with him, you'll find everything in order," said Strong.

"Very well," replied the voice crisply, and then added, "Remain where you are. Do not move from your present position or attempt to send any messages. If you fail to comply with these conditions you will be blasted!"

"Very well," said Strong, "conditions are understood."

"Boy," chimed in Roger, as he climbed down the ladder from the radar bridge, "they sure don't want any company here."

"And for good reason," said Strong. "The most vicious criminals in the whole universe are confined here. Every one of them is capable of committing any crime in the solar code. And most of them have. The men here are the worst. They have refused psychotherapeutic readjustment to make them into new men."

"But I thought they had to go through it, sir?" said Tom.

"No," replied Strong. "Even criminals have certain rights in our society. They can either remain criminals and stay here, or be psychoadjusted and given new personalities. The ones that refuse are the ones on this Rock."

"You mean," gasped Roger, "that the men on this asteroid deliberately chose to remain criminals?"

"Yes, Manning," said Strong. "Rather than become healthy citizens of the system, they prefer to stay here and waste their lives in isolation with no hope of ever returning to society."

"Can they change their minds after they get here?" asked Tom.

"Any time. But when they get this far, they usually stay here. The men on Prison Rock didn't surrender easily. They are the toughest, most ruthless men in the universe."

"Attention! Freighter *Dog Star*! Attention!" the audioceiver rasped into life again. "You have been given temporary clearance. A space launch will ferry you to the asteroid. You are warned that any weapons discovered on your person, or acts that may be construed as providing aid and comfort to the inmates of this prison, will be considered treason against the Solar Alliance and you will be subject to immediate disciplinary action."

Tom and Roger glanced at each other, a worried look in their eyes. Strong just smiled. "Don't worry, boys. That little speech is read to every visitor to the asteroid."

"Just the same, sir," said Roger huskily, "I would prefer to remain aboard the *Dog Star* and give you, Tom, and Astro the pleasure of the visit."

Strong laughed. "They won't let you, Roger. They'll send up a crew of guards to search the ship. And the way these boys search makes a customs inspection look like a casual glance."

"Attention *Dog Star*!" A younger voice suddenly came in on the audioceiver. "This is Lieutenant Williams aboard the space launch. We are approaching your starboard catapult deck. Please open the air lock and take us aboard."

"They sure don't waste any time," commented Tom as he turned to the audioceiver. "Freighter *Dog Star*, Cadet Tom Corbett to Lieutenant Williams," he called, "the air lock is open and the catapult deck is ready to receive you." At the same time, the young cadet turned the valve that would open the outer air lock to the jet-boat deck.

Five minutes later, the ship was swarming with tight-lipped enlisted Solar Guardsmen, who spoke to Strong and the cadets with cool courtesy. These were men who signed up for two years as guards on the Rock after competing with thousands of other enlisted men. A guard on the Rock was mid triple wages for the two-year isolation. But more than anything else the right to wear the bright white patch with a paralo-ray gun in the center denoting their service as guards on the Rock was prestige envied even by commissioned officers of the Solar Guard.

After what Tom thought to be the most thorough search he had ever seen was over, Lieutenant Williams reported to the control deck where Strong and the cadets had been politely but firmly detained. He informed them that they were now ready to blast off to the Rock, adding that a more detailed search of the area between the ship's outer and inner hulls would be conducted after they had gone.

"You mean," said Tom, amazed, "that you actually search the four inches between the two hulls? What in the universe could we possibly hide in there?"

"I don't know, Corbett," replied Williams. "We've never found anything there." He turned to Strong and smiled. "But there's always a first time, isn't there, sir?"

"Yes, of course," agreed Strong. "You do a thorough job, Williams. Very good indeed!"

"Thank you, sir," said Williams. "You know, we've heard about you and the *Polaris* unit here on the Rock." He turned to Tom, Roger, and Astro. "We have a stereo of that mercuryball game you played at the Academy when you were Earthworms."

"What?" cried Tom. "You mean that game was recorded?"

"It sure was," said Williams. "But we've seen it at least fifty times."

"Well, blast my jets!" said Astro in amazement.

The game was one that the cadets had played when they first entered the Academy. It had done much to unify the boys into a fighting team.

An enlisted sergeant suddenly appeared, snapping to attention in front of Lieutenant Williams. "Ready to blast off, sir," he said.

"Very well," said Williams, then turned to Strong and the cadets. "Follow me, please."

In a few moments the space launch was blasting away from

the freighter and heading for a tiny planetoid in the distance. As they drew near, Strong and the cadets peered out of the ports to get a view of the prison, but were disappointed when Williams ordered the ports covered.

He smiled apologetically at Strong and explained, "All approaches are secret, sir. We can't allow anyone to see where our defenses are located."

"You fellows certainly believe in keeping prisoners in and visitors out!" commented Strong.

"Anyone interested in coming to the Rock, sir," said Williams, "is under natural suspicion."

The three cadets gulped, duly impressed with the severity of the prison routine.

Soon they felt the unmistakable jar and bump of the small space vessel touching the surface of the planetoid. The jets cut out suddenly and Williams stood up.

"Please follow me. Do not speak to anyone, and do not stop walking. Keep your hands in front of you and maintain a distance of ten feet between you and the man in front of you."

He walked through the open hatch where a hard-faced enlisted guardsman stood rigidly, holding a paralo-ray gun at the ready.

With a quick nod to the cadets Strong followed Williams through the hatch. At ten-foot intervals they followed him out of the hatch, with Tom bringing up the rear and the enlisted guardsman behind him.

As Tom stepped out onto the surface of the asteroid he wasn't quite sure what he expected to see, but he certainly wasn't ready for the sight that greeted his eyes.

As far as he could see, there was grass, spotted with small one-story buildings. To the left was a single towering structure built of Titan crystal and on top of it was the largest atomic blaster he had ever seen. He turned to ask the guardsman about the gun but was motioned ahead with a curt, "No questions. Keep walking."

Tom continued to walk. He noticed that they were heading for the tower. As he drew nearer, he could see men walking around a narrow catwalk at the top. They all carried paralo-ray rifles with miniature grids mounted on the barrel. Inside the rifle was a tiny radar direction finder. It was a simple but effective control against escaping prisoners. Each of the inmates of the Rock wore small metal disks welded to a thin chain around their waists. The disk was sensitive to radar impulses, and with no more effort than snapping a thumb catch on the rifle, the guard could locate and paralyze the nearest disk-wearing inmate.

Tom was so full of questions it was necessary for the guard to warn him again, only this time in sharper tones.

Entering the tower, they were scrutinized and cleared by an electronic beam that passed through their bodies and indicated any metal they might carry. Once through this last barrier, they were escorted to a slidestairs, where Williams left them.

Throughout the entire procedure few words had passed between the cadets. Now left alone on the stairs, they couldn't contain themselves and the comments and questions tumbled out.

　　　　　　　　　Carey Rockwell

"Did'ja see that blaster on top of this place?" Roger blurted out.

"Those radar-controlled paralo-ray rifles are really something!" said Astro.

"The thing I want to know," said Tom, "is where are the prisoners? I haven't seen one yet."

"And you're not likely to, either, Cadet Corbett!" said a gruff voice above them. They turned to see a heavy-set man wearing the uniform of a major in the Solar Guard, standing on the floor above them. The slidestairs carried them to his level and Captain Strong hopped off and extended his hand in greeting.

"Major Savage!" he explained. "Good to see you again!"

"Same here," said Savage, returning Strong's firm handclasp. He turned and faced the cadets. "So this is the *Polaris* unit, eh?" He smiled. "We've really enjoyed the stereo of that game of mercuryball you played back at the Academy."

"Thank you, sir," said Tom. "Lieutenant Williams has already told us how much he liked it."

"Come into my quarters and relax. I imagine you could do with some good solid food after those synthetics on your trip."

"We certainly could, sir," said Strong.

They followed the big man through a sliding panel into a suite of comfortably furnished rooms. Five minutes later, the cadets and the officers were enjoying their first hot meal in a week. As they ate, Major Savage brought up the purpose of their visit. "So you've come to talk to Bull Coxine, eh?"

"Yes," nodded Strong. "And I don't imagine he has developed any affection for me."

"No, I wouldn't say he has," replied Savage. "In fact, I don't think Bull has any affection for anyone, not even himself. Why do you want to see him, anyway?"

Strong quickly summarized the theft of the adjustable light-key and the unsuccessful search for Wallace and Simms, concluding finally with the knowledge of Coxine's association with Wallace.

"I'm hoping Coxine will give me a lead to Wallace's whereabouts," said Strong.

"Well, you can ask him," shrugged the major. "But personally, I don't think you're going to get any further than saying hello. If he'll even let you say that. He hates you, Strong. Hates you in a way I've never seen a man hate before. When you talk to him, be careful."

"I will," said Strong grimly.

"Don't let him get near you. He's the strongest man I've ever seen. Came blasted near choking a guard to death with one hand when he escaped. He could break a man's neck with both hands."

Strong smiled. "Evidently, Major, you haven't noticed the size of Cadet Astro. I'll take him along with me for protection." He looked at Astro, who flushed in quick embarrassment.

"Very well, Strong," said Savage. "I'll have a jet car brought around. You can go right down to his hut."

"Er—may I ask a question, sir?" asked Tom.

The major smiled. "Go right ahead, Corbett."

"It's about this whole setup," explained Tom. "I was expecting fences and prisoners and—well, most anything but green grass and small white buildings!"

"The little huts you saw," replied the major, "are as much of a prison as we have. Each hut holds one prisoner. He has all the necessary furniture, in addition to audioceivers and story spools which he can change once a week. He also has basic garden equipment. All prisoners grow everything they eat. Each man is dependent on himself and is restricted to the hut and the area around it. If he comes within two miles of the tower, the guards will pick him up on radar and order him back. If he comes within one mile, they fire without further warning. Only one man has ever escaped. Coxine. And that was because we had a sick man on guard duty, or he never would have made it. He overpowered the guard, took his uniform, and stowed away on a supply ship. We caught him a year later."

"Didn't your radar pick up the disk he was wearing, sir?" asked Roger.

"That method of protection was only installed a few months ago," said the major.

"And the prisoners just sit there—in those little huts?" asked Astro.

"Yes, Astro!" said the major with a tone of finality in his voice. "They just sit. This is the end of the line."

The three cadets looked at each other and secretly vowed never to take a chance of doing anything that would send them to the Rock.

Five minutes later, Strong was driving a jet car along a narrow paved road toward one of the white huts. Astro sat beside him grimly silent, his hands balled into tight hamlike fists. They rounded a curve and Strong pulled up in front of the house. As they climbed out of the car, they could see the trim neat lanes of the little garden with carefully printed signs on each row indicating what was growing. They started for the house and then stopped short. Bull Coxine stood in the doorway, watching them.

Dressed in the snow-white coverall of the prison garb, Coxine faced them squarely, his thick trunklike legs spread wide apart. He was a giant of a man with long heavily muscled arms that dangled from a huge pair of shoulders. His jet-black hair was a tangled unkempt mass, and his face was scarred and lined. Eyes blazing with unconcealed hatred he waited for Captain Strong to make the first move.

"Hello, Bull," said Strong quietly. "I'd like to talk to you."

"Oh, you would, huh?" Coxine spat and his lips twisted in a mocking grin. "What's the matter? Afraid to talk to me alone?" he indicated Astro. "Did you have to bring one of your Space Cadets for protection?"

"Listen, Bull," urged Strong, "I was your friend once. I turned you in because you were a mutineer and I was an officer of the Solar Guard. I'd do the same to this cadet if he tried what you did."

"Yeah, I'll bet you would," snarled the criminal. "Just like a real friend!" His voice deepened into a low roar. "Don't talk

Carey Rockwell

to me about the old days! I'm on the Rock and you're just another Solar Guard space crawler to me. Now get out of here and leave me alone."

"I came to ask you to help me, Bull," Strong persisted. "I need information."

Coxine's eyes narrowed into slits. "What kind of information?"

"You once tried to hold up a Credit Exchange on Ganymede with a man called Gus Wallace. He had a hide-out in the asteroid belt. I'd like to know where it is," said Strong.

"Why?"

"I can't answer that, Bull."

"What do I get if I tell you?"

"Nothing, except my thanks and the thanks of the Solar Guard."

"And if I don't?"

"I'll turn around and leave."

"Then start turning, Strong," snarled the giant prisoner, "because I ain't got nothing to tell you except how much I hate your guts!"

Astro moved forward slightly, but Strong held him back. "O.K., Bull. If that's the way you want it, I'll leave."

"Why don't you let the young punk try something?" challenged Coxine. "I ain't had any exercise in a long time."

Strong looked at the huge man and said coldly, "I wouldn't want the death of a piece of space scum to show on his record."

Then, as if the space and sky overhead had suddenly been torn open, there was a flash of light followed by the roar of a tremendous explosion. The ground trembled. The air seemed to moan in agony. Strong and Astro wheeled around and looked toward the tower that shimmered in the light of the late afternoon sun. To their horror, they saw the unmistakable mushrooming cloud of an atomic blast rising in the synthetic atmosphere behind it.

"By the craters of Luna—" gasped Strong.

A second flash and explosion rocked the prison asteroid and suddenly the tower disappeared. Almost immediately, a spaceship appeared over the small planetoid and began systematically pounding the surface installations with atomic blasters.

"Captain Strong," cried Astro. "Tom and Roger—they were in the tower!"

"Come on," yelled Strong, "we've got to get back!"

"You ain't going nowhere, Strong," snarled Coxine behind him. "I've been waiting a long time for this!" He suddenly struck the Solar Guard officer with a heavy rock and Strong slumped to the ground unconscious. Before Astro could move, Coxine smashed him to the ground with a blow on the back of the neck. They both lay deathly still.

Then, as the atomic bombardment of the penal asteroid continued, the giant space criminal jumped into the jet car and sped away.

Carey Rockwell

CHAPTER 11

"Fire!" bawled Major Savage to his crew of gunners.

At the other end of the field one of the remaining two undamaged rocket destroyers blasted off to battle the invading spaceship.

Tom and Roger had been on a tour of the great central tower with Major Savage when the attack came and had been ordered to find safety in the open fields. The major knew the tower would be one of the first targets.

Sprawled on the ground behind a bunker, they saw the major, his space jacket torn from his back, standing in the middle of the field, quietly issuing orders to scarlet-clad spacemen, desperately trying to organize the penal asteroid's defenses.

The spaceship, which had somehow managed to penetrate the tight radar warning screen around the prison, had struck with merciless precision. Again and again, its atomic blasters had found the most important installations and had wiped them out. The first target, after the tower had been shattered, was the underground launching ramps for the asteroid's small fleet of rocket destroyers. But even after a direct hit, the guards were able to ready two ships to fight the attacking spaceship. The first was already diving in, her small one-inch blasters firing repeatedly.

Suddenly, Lieutenant Williams, in command of the second ship, came racing up to Major Savage, to report that his radarman had been hit and the ship couldn't blast off.

"Here's where I get into the act!" Roger jumped up immediately, and with a brief "So long, spaceman" to Tom, raced off to join Lieutenant Williams.

"Spaceman's luck," yelled Tom as the officer and the cadet ran toward the waiting ship.

Looking skyward again, Tom saw the first destroyer diving toward the attacking spaceship, trying to get in range with her lighter armament. Suddenly there was a burst of brilliant light. The lighter ship had been completely destroyed by a direct hit.

Sick with horror, Tom looked away and watched the ship Roger had joined blast off under full acceleration. It roared spaceward in a straight line, disappearing at incredible speed.

Meanwhile, the invader continued to blast relentlessly. One—two—three—four—automatic reload—one—two—three—four, reload. Over and over, firing at seemingly peaceful fields of grass, only to strike an armory, space cradle, or supply depot buried underneath the ground. Suddenly it changed its course and trained its guns skyward. Tom looked up and saw a tiny flyspeck roaring straight down at the ship. It was Lieutenant Williams' rocket destroyer, with Roger on the radar bridge, in a suicidal attempt to destroy the invader. But the larger ship was ready. The two forward blasters opened fire. A flaming ball of light exploded near the stabilizer of the destroyer and it fell off course to float helplessly in free-fall orbit around the asteroid. Still lying on the ground, Tom sighed with relief. At least Roger was all right.

Then the young cadet saw the invading spaceship move away from the area around the tower toward the horizon not too far away on the small planetoid. He followed it with his eyes and saw it suddenly land near a cluster of white prisoner huts. Tom gasped as the reason for the attack became clear.

"Major! Major! Major Savage!" he called as he raced across the field. But the major was nowhere to be seen. A guard carrying a medical kit hurried past him and Tom grabbed him by the arm.

"Major Savage! Where is he?"

The guard pointed to a near-by stretcher and Tom saw the unconscious figure of the major sprawled on the plastic frame.

"But—but the prisoners are getting away!" yelled Tom.

"I can't do anything about it. I've got wounded men to care for!" The man jerked away and disappeared in the smoky, choking dust.

The curly-haired space cadet, his face blackened from the smoke, his lungs crying for fresh air, started across the blast-pitted field, looking for help. But there was none to be had. Suddenly he wheeled in the direction of the spaceship and started to run toward it.

As soon as the young cadet had left the smoking area around the wrecked tower, he realized that it was the only section of the small satellite that had suffered attack. Ahead, he could see the prisoners in their white suits crowding around the stabilizer air lock of the invading ship.

Tom dropped to his stomach and watched the knot of men. Suddenly the air-lock portal slid open. There was a loud cheer and the prisoners began scrambling aboard.

Tom knew he would have to move fast. Taking a dangerous chance, he rose to a half-crouch and dashed to one of the small white huts only a hundred feet away. With a final glance at the thinning crowd of escaping men around the ship, he ran straight for an open window, diving headlong through it.

Inside, Tom waited breathlessly for a shout or warning that he had been seen, but none came. He glanced through the window and saw that only seven or eight men remained outside the port. He turned away quickly and began searching the hut.

He found what he was looking for rolled up on the bed where its owner had used it as an extra pillow. He shook out the prison suit of white coveralls, stripped off his own blue cadet's uniform, and hurriedly put on the distinctive prison gear. It was a little large for him and he rolled up the sleeves and trouser legs, hoping no one would notice in the excitement. Then, with a deep breath, he stepped out of the hut into full view of the prisoners still left at the air lock.

"Hey, wait for me!" he yelled, running for the ship.

The men paid no attention in their haste to get aboard the ship. When Tom reached the air lock, there were only two left. He slapped the nearest man on the back.

"Pal, I've been waiting for this a long time!"

Carey Rockwell

"Yah," the man answered, "me too!" Then he looked at Tom closely. "Say, I've never seen you around here before!"

"I just got in on the supply ship last week. They kept me in the tower for a while," Tom replied.

"Oh, well," said the man, "they ain't keepin' anybody there anymore!"

"Come on you guys," snarled a heavy-set man in the air lock above them. "We ain't got all day!"

Tom looked up, and without being told, he felt he was looking into the face of Bull Coxine. And when the other prisoner spoke, he was certain.

"Yeah, Bull," said the man. "Comin', comin'!" He reached up and Bull grabbed his outstretched hand. When Bull pulled, the man literally leaped through the air into the air lock.

"All right, space crawler," roared Bull to Tom, "you're next!" The big man stuck out his hand. Tom gulped. For one desperate second he thought of turning and running away.

"Well?" growled Bull. "You coming or ain't cha?"

"You're blasted right I'm coming," said Tom. "This is one time the Solar Guard is taking it on the chin. And, crawler, am I happy to see it!"

He grabbed Bull's hand and was lifted as easily as if he had been a feather. Coxine dropped him on the deck and turned away without a word to disappear inside the ship.

As he looked around, Tom suddenly felt a cold shiver run through his body. He felt as if he had signed his own death warrant. There was no mistake about it. The ship was the same one he had watched night after night at the exposition on Venus. And the names of the two owners exploded in his brain. "Wallace and Simms!"

He turned to jump out of the air lock, but it slid closed in front of him. He was trapped.

*   *   *   *   *

Sprawled on the ground in front of one of the white houses near the tower perimeter, Captain Strong stirred, shook his head, and painfully rose to a half-crouch. With eyes still dulled by shock, he looked around to see Astro lying unconscious a few feet away. His brain still reeling from the effects of Coxine's sneak attack, he staggered over to his knees beside him.

"Astro, Astro—" Strong called. "Astro, snap out of it!"

The big Venusian moaned and opened his eyes. He sat bolt upright. "Captain Strong! What happened?"

"I'm not too sure, Astro," said Strong. "All I remember is Coxine slugging me."

As they struggled to their feet, they suddenly noticed the towering columns of smoke rising into the air.

"By the rings of Saturn!" gasped Strong. "Look, Astro!"

"Blast my jets!" cried the big cadet. "What—what could have happened?"

The two spacemen stood gaping at the shattered remains of the tower and the smoldering area around it. In the distance,

Carey Rockwell

scarlet-clad guardsmen moved dazedly around the wreckage and above them a rocket destroyer was blasting on one jet, coming in for a touchdown.

"Astro," said Strong grimly, "I don't know how it could have happened, but the prison asteroid has been attacked. A rocket-blasting good job of it! Come on! We've got to get over there!"

"Yes, sir," said Astro. As they started running toward the field, he searched the figures moving about in the distance for two familiar blue uniforms. "I don't see Roger or Tom, sir," he said hesitantly. "Do you think—?"

"We'll just have to wait and see," interrupted Strong grimly. "Come on, step it up!"

As the two spacemen approached the smoking ruins of the underground cradles, ammunition dumps, and repair shops, they passed groups of men digging into the rubble. In sharp contrast to the careful scrutiny they had received when they first arrived at the prison, no one noticed them now. Strong stepped up to a man in a torn and dirty sergeant's uniform.

"What happened?" he asked.

The man turned and looked at Strong and Astro. Aside from the swollen bump on the Solar Guard captain's head and the bruise on the cadet's neck there were no signs of their having been in the attack. When the guardsman finally replied, there was a sharp edge to his voice. "I thought *everyone* knew we were attacked, *sir*!" He turned back to a detail of men who were watching. But Strong pulled the man up sharply.

"Attention!" he barked. The sergeant and the crew came to stiff attention. Strong stepped forward and looked the guardsman straight in the eye. "Under any other circumstances, Sergeant," snapped Strong, "I'd have your stripes and throw you in the brig for your insolence! Now I want a clear account of what happened. And I want it blasted *quick*!"

"Yes, sir!" stammered the guardsman, realizing he had gone too far. He hurriedly gave a detailed description of the battle, ending with a report that Major Savage had been injured and that Lieutenant Williams was now in command of the prison.

"Where will I find Lieutenant Williams?" asked Strong.

"At the rocket destroyer, sir. It just landed."

"Very well, Sergeant!" said Strong, adding in a gentler tone, "I realize you've had a rough time of it, so we'll forget what just happened. Get back to your work."

As Astro followed the Solar Guard captain toward the rocket ship he saw a familiar figure standing near the air lock. A boy with close-cropped blond hair and wearing cadet blues.

"Roger!" yelled Astro joyfully. "Captain Strong, look! It's Roger!"

They quickened their pace and were soon beside the small space vessel that had been blasted out of commission before it could fire a shot. While Roger was telling them of having volunteered for radar operations aboard the ship and of their being disabled by a near miss, Lieutenant Williams suddenly appeared in the air lock and saluted smartly.

"Major Savage has been injured, sir," said Williams. "Since you are the highest ranking officer on the asteroid, are there any orders?"

"I'm not acquainted with your men, or your prison, Williams," replied Strong. "I'll accept the command as a formality but appoint you my chief aid. Carry on and do anything necessary to get things cleared away."

"Very well, sir," said Williams.

"Have communications been destroyed?"

"Yes, sir. Communications was located in the tower, but Cadet Manning has converted the equipment on ship for long-range audio transmission."

"Very good!" said Strong. "As soon as you get a chance, I want you to make out a full report on the attack, including your personal opinion of who attacked us and why."

"I don't know who manned that ship, sir," said Williams, "but I can tell the reason all right. Every prisoner on the asteroid has escaped!"

"Yes," mused Strong. "I thought that would be the answer. But how did that ship get through your defenses?"

"Captain Strong," said Williams grimly, "I don't think there is any question about it. Someone broke the asteroid code. The attacking ship identified itself as the regular supply ship."

"A Solar Guardsman?" asked Strong.

"No, sir," said Williams. "I'd bet anything that none of our men would do that!"

"Then who?" asked Strong.

"Only one man would be smart enough to get the code and break it, and then sneak it off to the attacking ship!"

"Who?" asked Strong.

"Bull Coxine!" answered the young officer through clenched teeth.

They were interrupted by a guardsman. "Sir, we found this in prison hut twenty-four."

"What is it?" asked Strong.

Astro's eyes suddenly widened and he stepped forward. "Why, that's ... that's Tom's uniform!" he stammered.

"Tom!" gasped Strong. "But where is he?"

"We've searched the immediate area, sir," replied the guardsman. "Cadet Corbett isn't here."

"Are you sure?" demanded Strong.

"Yes, sir," said the guardsman stoutly.

Strong took the uniform and examined it carefully. Then he turned to Roger and snapped, "Prepare the audioceiver for immediate transmission to Space Academy, Manning. Astro! Get aboard our ship. Check her for damage and let me know how soon we can blast off!"

The two cadets saluted and raced for the small spaceship.

Thoughtfully holding Tom's uniform in his hand, Strong turned back to Williams. "I'm going to leave as soon as I can, Williams. I'll tell Space Academy about the attack and see that a relief ship is sent out to you right away. Meantime, I'm leaving you in command." He paused and looked at Tom's uniform again. "If Cadet Corbett isn't on the asteroid, he must be on the attacking ship with the prisoners. The only question now is, do they know it?"

"You mean he smuggled himself aboard?" asked Williams.

"I'm almost sure of it!" said Strong. "And if he *is*, he's going to try to get some sort of message out. I've got to be ready to pick it up."

Strong paused and looked up at the sky overhead, still thick with smoke. "And if he does ask for help, I'm going to answer him with the biggest fleet of spaceships he'll ever see in his life!"

CHAPTER 12

"Stand by, you space crawlers!" roared Bull Coxine into the microphone, but the loud laughter and singing of the noisily celebrating prisoners continued unabated over the intercom's loud-speakers. "Avast there!" he bellowed again. "Stow that noise! Attention! And I want *attention*!"

Standing on the control deck of his ship, Coxine waited as the men gradually quieted down. No longer wearing the white prison coverall, he was dressed in a black merchant spaceman's uniform, the snug-fitting jacket and trousers stretching tightly across his huge shoulders. He wore a black spaceman's cap, and two paralo-ray pistol belts were crisscrossed over his hips.

"Now listen to me!" he roared again. "Let's get one thing straight! I'm the skipper of this ship and the first man that thinks he's smarter than me, let him speak up!"

There was a long pause and the big man added with an ominous whisper, "But I warn you, if one of you opens your mouth, you'll take a swim in space!"

There was an angry murmur among the prisoners that Coxine heard over the intercom. "Don't think I can't take care of you, the lot of you, one by one or all at once. I cut my milk teeth

Carey Rockwell

on mutiny. I know how to start one and I know how to finish one! I needed a crew and that's the only reason you're here! Any spaceman that doesn't like the way I run things aboard this ship, better keep it to himself, or start swimming back to the prison asteroid!" He paused. "Well? Are you all with me?"

There was a chorus of cheers on the intercom and Coxine nodded grimly.

"All right," he continued, "now that we understand each other, I'll get on with the business. Second-in-command to me will be Gus Wallace. *Lieutenant* Wallace!"

A roar of approval came over the loud-speaker.

"Third-in-command—Luther Simms! *Lieutenant* Simms!"

There was another roar of approval as the prisoners recognized the names of the men who had liberated them from the asteroid.

"Now, we'll handle this ship as if it were any other freighter. The following men will be in charge of departments!"

As Coxine read off the list of jobs and the men to handle them, there were yells of approval and disapproval for favorites and old enemies. When the list of names had been read, he turned away from the intercom and faced his lieutenants, Wallace and Simms.

"Well, skipper," boasted Wallace, "it looks like we're in business again!"

"Yeah," chimed in Simms. "In three hours we'll be on our own asteroid and we can start planning our first strike!"

Coxine's eyes narrowed into slits. "Get this, both of you!" he snapped. "What I said to those crawlers down below goes for you too. I'm the boss of this outfit and you don't even guess about what we're going to do, until I say so!"

"But, Bull—!" whined Wallace.

"Shut up!" roared Coxine. "And when you talk to me, you call me captain!"

Wallace and Simms looked at each other. "O.K., Captain," muttered Simms.

"Yes, *sir*!" corrected Coxine.

"Yes, sir," said Simms quickly.

"That's better," growled the giant spaceman. "Don't get the idea that just because you were able to follow orders that it makes you smart. Because it doesn't! It took me two and a half years to get the information collected onto these story spools and smuggle them out to you. Everything, from where to buy this spaceship to getting the light-key out of the time capsule, was my idea! My brains!"

"Sure, Captain," said Wallace, "but we took the chances!"

"Yeah," sneered Coxine. "You took chances! The only chance you took was in not paying attention to what I told you to do. I gave it all to you. Where to hold up the first freighter passenger, what to take, how to mount the atomic blasters, what code to use in getting through the prison defenses. The whole works! And I did it while sitting on the toughest Rock in the system. I smuggled it out right under the noses of those Solar Guard space crawlers. So forget about being smart, or you'll wind up with that scum below decks!"

"Yes, sir!" said Wallace.

"Now get me a course to the asteroid and make it quick. And have some decent grub sent up to my quarters right away!"

The big man turned lightly on the balls of his feet and disappeared through the hatch. After a moment, Wallace turned to Simms.

"That big space-crawling bum!" snorted Wallace. "I oughta blast him!"

"Go ahead!" sneered Simms. "You were the one who wanted to get him off the Rock, not me!"

"Aw shut up!" snarled Wallace. He turned to the intercom and began barking orders to his new crew.

*   *   *   *   *

Tom Corbett sat in one corner of a cargo compartment that had been converted into sleeping quarters, watching the celebrating prisoners. Someone had broken into the galley stores and mixed a concoction of fruit, alcohol, and reactor priming fluid to make a foul-tasting rocket juice. The men sat about in various stages of undress as they changed from the white prison coveralls to the black uniforms of the merchant spaceman, and drank heavily from a huge pot of the liquid.

One of the men, short and stumpy, but with shoulders like an ape, was standing on a table boasting about his strength. He was stripped to the waist and Tom could see the powerful arms and chest beneath the black hair that covered his body. As he continued to brag, the prisoners laughed and jeered, calling him Monkey. The man's face reddened and he offered to fight anyone in the room. A short, thin man with a hawk nose sitting next to Tom yelled, "Monkey," and then darted behind a bunk. The man turned and looked angrily at Tom.

"You there!" the man on the table called, looking at Tom. "You call me Monkey?"

Tom shook his head. Since the blast-off he had stayed away from the men as much as he could, certain that sooner or later someone would challenge him and discover he wasn't a prisoner. He hoped to remain aboard the ship long enough to plant a signal for the Solar Guard to follow. Tom felt almost certain they would be heading for Wallace and Simms' hide-out. And so far, the men had been so excited over their new freedom they hadn't bothered him. He had managed to sit quietly in the corner of the storage compartment and watch them.

"I'm talking to *you*!" shouted the hairy man, looking straight at Tom. "You called me Monkey and then lied about it! Maybe you're scared, eh?"

He slipped off the table and advanced toward Tom. The young cadet tried to figure a way out of the threatening fight. He wasn't afraid of the man, but he didn't want to draw attention to himself. And one of the surest ways of letting Wallace and Simms know he was aboard ship was to get into a fight. He couldn't risk discovery. He had to signal the Solar Guard before he was caught. But how to get around the hairy, drunken criminal now standing over him?

Tom looked up and saw that the man would not be put off. He would have to fight. He took notice of the powerful arms and shoulders, and decided his best bet would be to stay away, but glancing around quickly he saw there wasn't any room to retreat. The other prisoners were crowding around, eager to watch the fight. Suddenly his opponent let out an animal-like roar and jumped to pin him down on the deck.

The young cadet timed his move perfectly. As the man's body came down on him, he threw up both legs and caught him in the pit of his stomach. Tom could feel his feet sink deep into the man's mid-section as he kicked out hard and sent him sprawling against the bulkhead. With a bellow of rage, the hairy man picked himself up and charged back at Tom, who was now on his feet, braced to meet him.

As the prisoners began to roar, Tom side-stepped and back-pedaled frantically, trying to get out of the impossible situation. If he won, there would be questions for him to answer. Questions that would be difficult and might betray his identity. But if he allowed Monkey to win, he might die right there on the deck. The man was blind with rage and would stop at nothing.

The man rushed in again and, unable to back away, Tom felt the hairy arms close around him in the most powerful grip he had ever felt in his life. Slowly, evenly, Monkey applied pressure. Tom thought his ribs would crack. His head began to swim. The faces around him that laughed and jeered suddenly began to spin around him dizzily.

Then, with the desperation of a man facing death, Tom began to push outward, his arms under Monkey's chin. The man tried to apply more pressure but the cadet fought him, forcing his head back farther and farther. The prisoners were silent, watching the deadly battle. Then, gradually, Tom felt the hairy man's grip relaxing. With the last ounce of his strength he burst out of the encircling arms and staggered back. The ape man looked at him stupidly and then down at his arms as if they had betrayed him. With a roar, he came rushing in again. Tom set himself, left foot forward, shoulders hunched, and when Monkey came within arm's length, he swung with all the strength he had left in his body. His fist landed on the point of Monkey's chin. There was a distinct sound of crushing bone and Monkey sank to the deck, out cold. Gasping for breath, Tom stood over the sprawled man and just looked at him. The crowd around him was staring at the fallen man in disbelief. Through the roaring in his head, Tom could hear their voices, "He broke out of Monkey's grip!" "He broke the guy's jaw with one punch!"

Tom turned blindly to the corner where he had been sitting and slumped to the deck. Someone shoved a cup in his hands and he gulped its contents blindly, hardly tasting the foul rocket juice or feeling it burning his throat.

The cadet was sure now that he would be caught. Monkey had been a popular member of the crew and some of his friends were certain to even the score. But to Tom's surprise, there were no questions and a few of the men came over to pat him drunkenly on the back. A couple of them dragged the unconscious man out of the compartment and up to sick bay. The others soon forgot the fight and continued their merrymaking.

Tom sat alone and silent in the corner, his strength returning slowly. He had faced his first obstacle and had won. But he knew that what lay ahead of him made the fight insignificant by comparison. He decided his next move would be to acquaint himself with the ship and, if possible, get a paralo-ray gun.

As the men continued their drunken singing and yelling he mumbled an excuse about soaking his fist in cold water and managed to escape from the crowded compartment.

Carey Rockwell

Outside in the passageway, the cadet began to figure out the plan of the ship, first locating the power deck by its roaring purr. He climbed a ladder to the next deck, walked slowly down the passageway toward what he thought to be the control room, and leaned against the hatch. He heard the soft tinkle of a radar signal and his heart skipped a beat. He had stumbled onto the astrogation and radar bridge. Wondering if he should burst into the room and attempt to overpower the men on duty, or wait for a better chance later, he was suddenly startled by a sharp voice in back of him.

"You—spaceman!" Tom turned to stare right into the face of Bull Coxine!

The big man looked at Tom with piercing eyes.

"What's your name?" demanded Coxine.

"Uh—uh—they call me the Space Kid!" he finally managed.

"Space Kid, eh?" mused Coxine. "I don't remember seeing you on the Rock."

"They held me in the tower for a month trying to make me take the psychograph rehabilitation. I got out when the blasting started."

"What were you on the Rock for?" asked Coxine. "You're pretty young to be sent to the Rock."

Tom thought desperately of a crime he could have committed that would send him to the prison asteroid. Suddenly he got an idea. He looked at Coxine and spoke in as harsh a voice as he could.

"Listen," he snarled, "I just broke Monkey's jaw for treating me like a kid. I hope you don't crowd me into fighting you by asking so many questions. Y'see I won't answer them and then you'll have to freeze me." Tom paused and tried to gauge Coxine's reaction. But he couldn't see a thing in the cold staring eyes. "And," Tom continued, "if you freeze me, you'll lose a better man than most of the scum in your crew!"

Coxine stepped forward and towered over the curly-haired cadet. When he spoke, his deep voice echoed in the deserted passageway.

"What was your rating as spaceman before you hit the Rock?" asked the big man.

Tom's heart raced. If he could get to the control deck or the radar bridge, he could send his signal easily. But he realized quickly that in either of these places he would be spotted almost immediately by Wallace or Simms. He had to stay away from them and wait for a later chance. Tom's mind raced.

"I was a gunner on a deep spacer," he drawled confidently. "I can take the space tan off a crawler's nose at a hundred thousand yards with anything from a two-inch to a six-inch blaster."

Coxine's eyes sharpened. "Where did you learn to use a six-incher? They're only on heavy cruisers of the Solar Guard!"

Tom could have bitten his tongue off. He had slipped. He thought quickly. "I was an enlisted spaceman in the Solar Guard."

"Why'd you get sent to the Rock?"

"My officer was a smart-alec lieutenant just out of Space

Academy. We got in a fight—" Tom didn't finish the sentence.

"And you were kicked out, eh?"

"No, sir," said Tom. "I hit him so hard—he never woke up again. I had to blast out of there, but they caught me."

"All right," said Coxine. "Report to the gunnery chief. Tell him I said you're second-in-command." The big man turned and walked away from the cadet without another word.

Tom watched him disappear and smiled. He had faced two impossible situations, the fight with Monkey and now this meeting, and he had come out on top in each. Perhaps he had a chance, after all.

CHAPTER 13

"Any report from the search squadrons yet, Steve?" asked Commander Walters.

"No, sir," replied Captain Strong. "We're concentrating on the asteroid belt, but so far we've drawn a blank."

"Well, keep trying and let me know the minute something turns up," said Walters.

"Yes, sir," said Strong, saluting his commanding officer as the elder spaceman left the room. He turned back to a large desk in the center of the room where Roger Manning was busy noting figures on a large chart, showing the areas already covered and listing the squadrons engaged in the search.

As Strong leaned over his shoulder, Roger placed a finger on the chart. "Squadron Ten has just completed a search of all asteroids in their assigned area," he said, then added laconically, "Nothing."

Strong studied the chart a moment. "Well, we'll have to keep it up," he said. "It's the only way we'll find them. A systematic search of the belt from end one to the other." He paused and then muttered, "Only one thing I'm worried about."

Carey Rockwell

"What's that, sir?" asked Roger.

"That when we do find them, it'll be too late to help Tom."

"You really think he's aboard Coxine's ship, Captain Strong?"

"Couldn't be anywhere else," answered Strong. "And he'll be trying to signal us, you can bet on that. Keep me posted on all radar contacts made by the search squadrons. I want a continuous six-way radar sweep by every ship."

"Yes, sir," said Roger.

"One more thing," said Strong, "tell Astro to get the *Polaris* ready to blast off. And you make sure your radar bridge is in A-one condition."

"Are we blasting off, sir?" asked Roger.

"Every ship we can get into space will give us a better chance of finding Coxine and his crew. Now that we've got the search fully under way there's no need to hang around here any longer."

"Glad to hear it, sir," replied Roger. "I was getting a little itchy to hunt for those crawlers myself. And Astro can hardly keep still."

Strong smiled. "Don't worry, we'll find Tom," he said. "Wherever he is, you can bet he's taking care of himself and doing a good job for the Solar Guard."

Roger's eyes twinkled. "Oh, I wasn't so worried about Tom as I was Astro, sir. He'll be pretty mad if there isn't anything left of Coxine to pay him back for slugging him."

Strong rubbed his head and said grimly, "Astro's not the only one!"

The blond-haired cadet left the room, and Strong wearily turned back to study the chart of the search in the asteroid belt.

Immediately upon arrival at Space Academy, two days before, Strong had been placed in charge of the search by Commander Walters. The attack on the prison asteroid and the escape of the prisoners had created the biggest sensation in his life. From one end of the Solar Alliance to the other, the visunews and the stereos were full of the attack and escape details, with Strong's name appearing often in the headlines and news flashes. To search the asteroid belt had been his suggestion, and while he could offer no proof, he believed the attacking ship had been commanded by Wallace and Simms. Speaking only to Commander Walters, Strong had received permission to combine the search for Wallace and Simms, with the new hunt for Coxine. Strong was convinced that Coxine was behind the activity of Wallace and Simms, from the beginning at the Solar Exposition to the present.

Strong looked at his watch. It was past midnight. He flipped a switch and paged Lieutenant Moore on the central communicators. In a few moments the young officer appeared and saluted smartly.

"Take over here, Moore," said Strong. "I'm going to sack in for a little rest and then take the *Polaris* out. I'll be in constant contact with you and will direct search operations from the *Polaris*. You stand by here and relay all reports. We'll use code 'VISTA' for all contacts."

"Yes, sir," said Moore. "Shall I work up charts like that

one?" He pointed to the chart left by Roger.

"Statistics here at the academy will handle that," replied Strong. "Just shoot the information down to them as you receive it. And you'd better get someone else up here to help you. You'll be here a long time."

Moore saluted and Strong walked wearily from the room. There wasn't any need for cleverness now, thought the Solar Guard captain. When we catch Coxine, he'll fight. And when he fights, that will be the end of him!

He went to his quarters and in thirty seconds was asleep.

*   *   *   *   *

"Radar bridge to control deck!" A voice crackled over the intercom aboard the newly named pirate ship, *Avenger.* "Hullo, control deck! Come in!"

"Yeah?" roared Bull Coxine. "Whaddya want?"

"Picked up a blip on the radar, Captain," replied the radar officer. "Looks to me like the jet liner from Mars to Venus."

"Relay the pickup to the control-deck scanner and let me take a look at it," ordered Coxine.

In a moment the big pirate was studying the scanner carefully. Wallace and Simms stood to one side. Coxine turned and looked at them with a hard glint in his eyes. "That's the jet liner, all right!" He rubbed the palms of his huge hands together and smiled thinly. "It looks like we're in business!"

Wallace stepped forward. "You mean, you're going to—?"

"I'll tell you what I mean," snapped Coxine, "when I want you to know it!"

He turned to the intercom and began to bawl orders into the microphone.

"All hands! Stand by your stations for attack!"

There was an answering roar of approval from the crew.

"We're making our first strike, you space crawlers! A jet liner from Mars to Venus. There'll be lots of fancy things aboard her. Things the Solar Guard wouldn't give you on the Rock!"

There was another roar over the loud-speaker.

"But the first man that takes anything but what I tell him will find himself on the wrong end of two big fists!"

"We're closing in, Captain," interrupted the voice from the radar bridge. "The angle of approach is in our favor. I don't think they've seen us yet!"

"Keep watching her, Joe," replied Coxine, and turned to his two henchmen on the control deck. "You, Wallace! Take number-one jet boat. Russell, Stephens, Attardi, and Harris. Each man will take a paralo-ray pistol and rifle. Report to your boat when I give the order."

There was a pause as the men named scurried to their stations. Coxine continued, "The following men will come with me in boat number two. Shelly, Martin, and the Space Kid. The rest of you man the forward and aft blasters. But no one fires until Lieutenant Simms gives the order!"

Carey Rockwell

He turned to Simms and stared at the man coldly. "I'll be in contact with you all the time. You'll fire when I say to fire, and not before. Is that clear?"

Simms nodded.

"Range-fifty thousand yards to liner, Captain!" reported the radar bridge. "I think she's sighted us!"

"Forward turret!" roared Coxine. "Put a blast across her bow just to show how friendly we are!"

"Aye, aye, sir," acknowledged a voice from the gun turret.

In the turret Tom listened to the orders to attack the helpless spaceship with mounting anxiety. If he could only plant the signal on the *Avenger* before going to the liner, he might be able to remain aboard the passenger ship and escape. He was interrupted in his thoughts by a rough voice in back of him.

"Hey, Kid! Space Kid!" yelled Gaillard, the commander of the gun turret. "Come on! You heard the orders, didn't you? Get me the range."

"Right away," answered Tom. He stepped to the range finder, quickly figured the speed of the jet liner, their own speed and the angle of approach. Racking them up on the electronic tracker, he turned back to Gaillard, "Let her go!"

"Fire!"

There was a thunderous noise and the *Avenger* rocked gently in recoil from the heavy blast. Tom quickly sighted on the range finder and saw a ball of light flash brilliantly in front of the passenger ship. He breathed a sigh of relief. He had to keep up his avowed reputation of being a crack marksman and at the same time could not damage the unarmed passenger ship. The shot had been perfect.

"Good shooting, Kid," roared Coxine from the control deck.

"Thanks, skipper," said Tom, aware that he had not called Coxine captain, but knowing that his earner speech to the giant pirate had earned him a certain amount of respect.

Coxine quickly made contact with the captain of the liner on the teleceiver and the outraged captain's face sharpened into focus on the screen aboard the *Avenger*.

"By the craters of Luna," exploded the skipper of the passenger ship, "what's the meaning of this? There are women and children aboard this vessel."

Coxine smiled thinly. "My name's Bull Coxine, master of the vessel *Avenger*. One funny move out of you and I'll blast your ship into protons! Stand by for a boarding party!"

"Captain! Captain!" the radar operator's voice screamed over the control-deck loud-speaker, "they're trying to send out a signal to the Solar Guard!"

"They are, huh?" roared Coxine. "Forward turret, check in!"

"Turret, aye!" reported Tom. He had been left alone while Gaillard issued small arms to the boarding parties.

"Listen, Kid!" roared Coxine. "You said you're a good shot. Right now is the time to prove it. Blast away her audio antenna!"

Tom gulped. At a range of fifty thousand yards, the antenna, a thick piece of steel cable, might as well have been a needle to hit.

"Right, skipper," he finally replied. "I'll show you some of the fanciest shooting you'll ever see in your life!"

He turned back to the range finder, his mind racing like a calculating machine. He figured the angles of the two ships, considering that the jet liner was a dead ship in space and the *Avenger* still under way, but slowing down at a specific rate of deceleration. He rechecked his figure a third and fourth time, correcting his calculations each time with the forward movement of the *Avenger*. If he misjudged a fraction of a degree, he might kill or injure hundreds of people aboard the passenger vessel.

"Well?" roared Coxine. "Are you going to fire or not?"

"Coming right up, skipper!" shouted Tom. "Watch this!"

Steeling himself, lest he should hit the ill-fated ship, he fired. For a brief moment he felt sick and then heard the roar of the pirate captain from the control deck.

"By the rings of Saturn," roared Coxine, "that was the best shot I've ever seen! Well done, Kid! All right, boarding crews! Man your boats and stand by to blast off!"

While Coxine vocally lashed the members of the murderous crew into action, Tom tried to figure out some way to get to the radar deck unseen. Being assigned to the jet boat with Coxine, instead of Wallace, had been a lucky break and Tom wished for a little more of the same. Lining up with his boarding crew, he received his paralo-ray pistol and rifle from Gaillard, deftly stealing a second pistol while the gunnery officer's back was turned.

After hurriedly hiding the stolen gun, he slipped stealthily topside to the radar bridge. Reaching the hatch, he was about to open it, when he heard footsteps. He turned and saw a man walking toward him. It was Simms!

"Where in the blasted universe is the jet-boat deck?" snarled Tom. He dropped his rifle on the deck and bent over to pick it up, hiding his face.

"You're on the wrong deck," said Simms. "Two decks below. Get moving!"

The pirate lieutenant hardly gave the cadet a glance as he brushed past and entered the radar bridge. Tom caught a fleeting glimpse of the interior. His heart jumped. The bridge was exactly like the one on the *Polaris*! Though annoyed that his chance had slipped past, Tom was thankful to learn that the communications equipment was thoroughly familiar.

"Space Kid! Report to the jet-boat deck on the double!" Coxine's voice rumbled through the empty passageway. Tom dashed down the nearest ladder and hurried to the jet-boat deck where the pirate captain waited impatiently.

"I was checking the range and setting up to blast the liner in case they try anything funny," explained Tom. "I don't trust anyone on that range finder but me!"

Coxine chuckled. "Good work, Kid. I like a man that thinks ahead. Maybe I made the wrong man gunnery chief." He climbed into the jet boat. "All right, take the controls, Kid. Shelly and Martin, get in the stern." The men climbed in and Tom slid under the controls and waited for the order to blast off.

Wallace and his crew were on the opposite side of the ship,

so Tom had no fear of being recognized until they were all on the passenger ship. At his side, Coxine spoke to Wallace in the other jet boat over the audioceiver.

"We'll split up. I'll handle the control deck and you go aft to the supply lockers. Dump everything out in space and we can pick it up later. Search the passengers, but no rough stuff. The first man that puts his hands on anyone will never know what hit him!"

Tom listened to the pirate captain's orders and was forced to give the man credit for his tight control over his murderous crew. However rebellious he might be against the Solar Guard, and whatever it was that made the man become the system's most notorious criminal, his orders spoke for themselves.

"All right, Kid," roared Coxine, "blast off!"

Tom pressed the control pedal at his foot and the small ship shot out into the black void of space. Ahead of them, thousands of yards away, he could see the gleaming passenger ship.

In a few moments the two jet boats were braking their jets and drifting to a stop inside the catapult deck of the luxurious liner.

Almost before Tom had stopped the small craft, Coxine was out of the boat waving his paralo-ray pistols at a cluster of frightened merchant spacemen.

"Back inside!" he snarled. "Kid! Shelly! Cover me! We're going to the control deck. Martin, you stay here with the jet boat."

Coxine marched straight through the ship, head up, eyes straight ahead, while behind him, Tom and Shelly swept the luxurious lounges with their ray rifles, ready to fire on any who dared resist. They marched past the frightened passengers, climbed a flight of carpeted stairs to the next deck, and entered the control room.

The liner's captain, a tall, thin man with graying hair, stood waiting beside the control panel, his eyes flashing angrily. A half-dozen junior officers stood stiffly in back of him.

Coxine stepped up to the elderly officer and laughed good-naturedly. "No one will be hurt, skipper. I just want a few things for my men"—he paused and glanced at the ship's vault—"and whatever you have in there!"

"I'll live to see the day when you're caught and sent to the prison asteroid for this," snorted the captain.

"Don't make me laugh, skipper," said Coxine lightly. "The Solar Guard will have to build a new one for me. Don't think there's much left of the old one!"

"Then it was you! You're responsible for the attack on the asteroid!"

Coxine just smiled and turned to Tom and Shelly. "Watch these crawlers closely, now. I'm going to open the vault."

Tom stared at the ship's officers, hoping to catch the eye of one of them, but they were all watching Coxine.

The pirate captain pulled a thin rod about two feet long, with a switch on one end, from his jacket. He walked to the solid titanium door of the vault and inserted the rod into a small hole, pressing the switch at the end of the rod carefully several times. He stepped back and inserted it in another hole in the face of the door and repeated the procedure. Putting the key back in his jacket he grabbed the handle of the massive door. It swung open at his touch. The captain of the liner and officers gasped in amazement.

Working quickly, Coxine crammed the thick bundles of credit notes and passenger's valuables into a bag. At last he straightened up, and facing the unbelieving officer again, he tossed them a mocking salute. He nodded to Tom and Shelly and walked out of the control room without another word.

Shelly and Tom quickly followed the giant spaceman back to the jet-boat deck, where Wallace was just returning from his own operations. Wallace made a circle out of his fingers to Coxine and the giant pirate nodded.

"Let's get out of here!" he ordered.

"Aren't you afraid they'll try to stop you, skipper?" asked Tom.

Coxine laughed. "Just let them try. I never met a man yet that had the nerve to pull the trigger of a paralo-ray gun while my back was turned."

Tom gulped and wondered if he would have the nerve to fire on the spaceman. He thought about it a moment and decided that he would take any chance that came along, if he could outwit the criminal. When the time came, he would risk his life to stop Coxine!

CHAPTER 14

"All right, line up, you space crawlers!" bawled Coxine. "When I call your name step up to get your share of the haul!"

The pirate captain was seated at the head of a long mess table, an open ledger in front of him. There were stacks of crisp new credit notes at his elbow. He took out his paralo-ray pistols and placed them within easy reach. On either side of him, Wallace and Simms sat, staring at the money with greedy eyes.

Coxine looked at the first name on the ledger.

"Joe Brooks!" he called. "One thousand credits for spotting the liner!"

Brooks grinned and amid cheers walked to the table. Coxine handed him a small stack of notes carelessly and turned back to the ledger.

"Gil Attardi!" he roared. "One thousand credits for working on the boarding crew."

Attardi, a sly, scar-faced man, stepped forward to accept his share. He carried a long, thin knife with an edge so deadly

Carey Rockwell

keen that he could and often did shave with it.

Coxine continued his roll call. "Sam Bates! Five hundred credits. Straight share."

Bates stepped forward and glared at Coxine.

"How come I only get five hundred and the others get a thousand?" he snarled. "It ain't my fault I'm stuck on the power deck while you grab all the glory jobs!"

The laughing, excited crowd of men grew silent as the rebellious spaceman faced Coxine.

"You get five hundred credits," snarled Coxine. "Take it or leave it!"

"I want the same as Brooks and Attardi," demanded Bates.

Quicker than the eye could follow, Coxine rose and smashed the man in the face with a giant fist. Bates dropped to the deck like a stone. Coxine glared at the rest of the crew.

"The next crawler that thinks he's not getting his fair share," he snarled, "will get a trip in space for his share!" He glanced down at the unconscious man and jerked his thumb toward the hatch. "Get him out of here!"

Two men dragged the unconscious man away and threw a bucket of cold water on him. He woke up, snatched at his share of the credits, and disappeared from the room.

The pirate captain continued reading the list of names, arbitrarily, handing out various amounts of the stolen money as he saw fit.

Standing in the rear of the messroom, hidden by the other members of the crew, Tom realized that to step in plain sight of Wallace and Simms for his share would mean instant betrayal. He had to make his move now, and with most of the crew mustered together in the messroom, it was his one chance for success.

Gripping the stolen paralo-ray gun in his jacket pocket, he slipped out of the messroom unnoticed and headed for the radar bridge.

As he raced up the companionway he could hear the laughter of the men below decks as one by one they received their shares. His name would be called soon. Heart pounding, he stopped outside the radar hatch, pulled the paralo-ray gun from his jacket, and taking a deep breath opened the hatch.

Joe Brooks was seated in front of the scanner counting his share greedily and glancing occasionally at the finger of light that swept across the green globe. When Tom opened the hatch, he looked up and smiled.

"Hiya, Kid," he said. "Coxine's all right. I got a thousand just for picking up that ship on the radar. How much did you collect?"

"This," said Tom. He shoved the paralo-ray gun into Brooks' stomach. The man gulped and finally found his voice.

"Say, what is this? A gag? Where did you get that paralo-ray?" Then suddenly he shoved the bundle of notes in his pocket. "Oh, no, you don't! You're not going to steal my share!"

"I don't want your money!" said Tom coldly. "Get into that

locker and keep your mouth shut, or I'll blast you!"

"Locker? Say, what's the matter with you? You gone space happy?"

"Get in there," growled Tom. At the look on the cadet's face, Brooks rose quickly and stepped into the locker. Tom slammed the door and locked it. Then, locking the passageway hatch, he turned to the radar scanner. Working quickly with deft hands, he opened the casing around the delicate instrument and began disconnecting the major terminals. Studying the complicated tangle of connections, he wished that he had as much knowledge of radar as Roger.

He finally found the wires he wanted and separated them from the other connections. He began replacing them, altering the terminals. After checking his work, to make sure it would not short-circuit, he grabbed the intercom and began taking it apart. Sweat beaded his forehead. Time was short. Soon Coxine would miss him and come looking for him. He had to complete his job before that happened.

After moments that seemed like hours he was ready. Using one of the intercom relays he began tapping out a message in Morse code on an exposed wire from the scanner. He looked at the radar scanner and watched it flash white static lines each time he touched the wires. Carefully he tapped out a message.

" ... emergency ... attention ... Corbett ... Space Cadet ... aboard ... Coxine ... pirate ... ship ... space quadrant ... B ... section ... twenty ... three ..."

Over and over he repeated the desperate message, hoping against hope that someone would be scanning space and the interference would show up on their radar.

" ... emergency ... attention ... Corbett ... Space Cadet—"

* * * * *

"Captain Strong!" Roger's voice came shrieking over the ship's intercom. "Captain! Quick! I'm picking up a message from Tom!"

"What?" cried the Solar Guard officer. "Nail it! I'm coming up!"

Scrambling up the ladder to the radar bridge from the control deck, Captain Strong rushed over to the scanner and watched eagerly as blinking flashes washed out the background of the screen.

Slowly, at times unevenly, the message flashed and the two spacemen read it with gladdening hearts. Strong made a careful note of the position while Roger continued to read the flashes. Turning to the astrogation panel, the Solar Guard captain quickly plotted a course that would bring them to Tom's position.

Endlessly, during the past few days, Strong, Roger, and Astro had swept space in a wide arc around the asteroid belt, hoping to pick up just such a signal. Now, with the position of the *Avenger* in his hands, Strong grabbed for the intercom.

"Attention, power deck!" yelled Strong. "We've just picked up a message from Tom. He's given us his position, so stand by for a course change."

"Yeee-eooow!" roared Astro. "I knew he'd do it."

"He's not in the clear yet. We've only got his position. We don't know how we're going to get him away from Coxine yet."

"Ready to change course, sir," said Astro.

"Three degrees on the down-plane of the ecliptic, and fifty-four degrees to starboard. Full space speed, Astro! Pile it on!"

"Aye, aye, sir!" replied Astro. "I'll make this wagon's tail so hot it'll blast at double speed!"

"You'd better, you Venusian ape!" cried Roger. "It's the least you can do for Tom!"

"Stow it, Manning," growled Astro good-naturedly, "or I'll stick some of your hot air in the jets for extra power!"

"Cut the chatter, both of you!" snapped Strong. "Astro, execute course change!"

Astro's reply was a blast on the steering rockets. On the control deck, Strong watched the needle of the astral compass swing around and stop dead on the course he had ordered.

"All set, Astro!" shouted Strong. "Right on course. Now pile on the neutrons!"

"Aye, aye, sir."

On the power deck, the big cadet turned to his control panel, took a deep breath, and opened the reactant feeders wide. The ship leaped through the airless void under the sudden burst of power and Astro watched the acceleration indicator climb to the danger line. He gulped as the needle passed the danger point and was about to cut down speed when the needle stopped. Astro breathed easily and settled back satisfied. If it was up to him, they would reach Tom in record time.

Up on the radar deck, Roger continued to read the flashing signals on the radar scanner. Over and over, he read the same message.

"I guess that's all he can say, sir," said Roger, turning to Strong.

"Yes, I guess so, Roger," agreed Strong. "He's probably sending it out blind, on an open circuit, hoping that anyone near enough would pick it up. Wonder how he did it?"

Roger thought a moment. "I'm not sure, sir, but I think he's crossed the impulse on the scanner from positive to negative."

"How do you mean?" asked Strong. The young captain was well acquainted with the principle of radar but, admittedly, could not match Roger's natural ability.

"By making the impulse negative, sir," said Roger, "he could create interference on the scanner. Instead of bouncing against something and returning an image to a scanner, the impulse hits itself and creates static which shows up in the form of those white flashes."

"Well, in any case," said Strong with a sober nod toward the scanner, "he's done something the whole Solar Guard couldn't do. He's quite a boy!"

Roger smiled. "I'll say he is, skipper!"

Strong turned away and climbed down to the control deck. He sat in front of the great control panel and watched the countless dials and needles. But his mind wasn't on the delicate handling of the great ship. He was thinking about Tom, alone aboard a ship with a crew of desperate criminals.

Carey Rockwell

Tom had taken his life in his hands to send out the message, that much Strong was sure of! And the young skipper noted with pride that there was no appeal for help in the desperate call.

He shook his head wearily and flipped the teleceiver switch to report to Commander Walters.

* * * * *

"Emergency ... attention...." Tom continued to tap out the message slowly and carefully. Behind him, he could hear Brooks hammering against the locker door. Tom felt like opening the door and freezing the pirate with his paralo-ray gun to keep him quiet, but he didn't dare to stop sending.

Finally Tom decided it was time to go. "If anyone's going to pick up the message," he thought, "they've picked it up by now. I may still have time to get away in a jet boat."

He tied the wires together, causing a continuous interference to be sent out, and secured the radar casing. "If I'm lucky enough to get away in a jet boat," thought Tom, "at least they won't be able to pick me up on that!"

Without a glance at the locker where Brooks continued to pound and yell, Tom turned to the hatch leading to the passageway. He gripped the paralo-ray gun and opened the hatch. Peering into the passageway and finding it deserted, he slipped out and closed the hatch behind him. From below, he could hear the roar of the crew as the last of them received his share of the stolen credits.

Tom raced down the companionway toward the jet-boat deck. He made the first deck safely and was about to climb down to the next when he was spotted by Attardi, the scar-faced spaceman, who stood at the bottom of the ladder.

"Hey, Kid!" Attardi shouted. "The skipper's been looking for ya. You got the biggest cut. Three thousand credits for that fancy shooting you did!"

Tom noticed the gleam of the knife at the man's side. The young cadet could imagine the criminal sinking the knife in his back without hesitation, if he suspected anything.

"Well," demanded Attardi, "are you going to collect or not? The skipper sent me to look for you."

Tom smiled, and while still smiling, whipped the paralo-ray gun into sight and fired. His aim was true. Attardi froze, every nerve in his body paralyzed. He could still breathe and his heart continued to beat, but otherwise, he was a living statue, unable to even blink his eyes.

Tom jumped past the spaceman and dashed for the jet-boat deck. He had to hurry now. Attardi would be discovered any moment and be neutralized. When neutralized, the victim returned to normal, with only violent muscle soreness remaining.

Tom reached the jet-boat deck, opened the hatch, and raced for the nearest small craft. Suddenly from behind he could hear the buzz of a paralo-ray on neutralizing charge. Attardi had been discovered.

Tom jumped into the nearest jet boat, closed the hatch, and pressed the button releasing the sliding side of the ship's hull. Slowly, the great wall of metal slid back exposing the cold black velvet of deep space. As soon as the opening was wide enough, Tom pressed the acceleration lever and the small ship shot out, its jets roaring.

Carey Rockwell

Tom quickly glanced around to locate his position by the stars and saw that he was close to the asteroid belt. He opened up to full acceleration, and since there was nothing else to do but wait for time to pass and hope for escape, he began to examine the contents of the small ship. He opened the emergency food locker and was relieved to see it fully stocked with synthetics and water. Every second carried him farther away from the *Avenger*, and when he looked back, Tom saw no evidence of pursuit. The cadet smiled. They would depend on the radar to find him, instead of sending out the other jet boats. Tom almost laughed out loud. With the radar jammed, he was safe. He would make it. Once inside the asteroids, they would never find him.

Glancing around the few indicators on the control board of the small vessel, Tom's smile changed to a grimace of sudden terror. The jet boat had not been refueled after their raid on the jet liner. There was less than three days' oxygen remaining in the tanks. In three days the jet boat would become an airless shell. A vacuum no different than the cold silent void of space!

CHAPTER 15

"What's our position, Roger?" Captain Strong called into the intercom.

"Space quadrant B, section twenty-three, sir," replied Roger from the radar bridge. "But I can't see a thing on the radar. That static flash Tom sent out is scrambling everything."

"But you're sure this is our position?"

"Yes, sir. I checked it three times."

"All right, then," said Strong grimly. "There's only one thing to do. We're too near the asteroid belt to use the *Polaris* without radar, so we'll search in jet boats. Astro! We're parking right here! Give me full braking rockets and secure the power deck. Then prepare the jet boats for flight."

"Aye, aye, sir," came the reply from the Venusian.

The ship bucked under the tremendous power of the braking rockets and came to a dead stop in space. Strong dashed up the ladder to the radar bridge where Roger was still hunched before the radar scanner.

"Any chance of switching the scanner to another frequency

Carey Rockwell

and offsetting the effects of the static, Roger?" asked the Solar Guard captain.

Roger shook his head. "I don't think so, sir. The interference would have to be eliminated at its source."

"Well," sighed Strong, "to go looking for Tom without the help of radar would be like looking for an air bubble in the ammonia clouds of Jupiter. And we don't even know if he's still aboard the *Avenger* or not!"

"You know, sir," said Roger speculatively, "I've been thinking. I might be able to get a fix on this interference."

"A fix? How?"

"By blanking out the radar range, so that it would only work at one point of the compass at one time, then testing each heading separately until the flash appears. When it does, we'd at least know in which direction to blast off and trail Coxine.

"If you can do that, Roger," exclaimed Strong, "it would take us right into Coxine's lap! Do you think you can work it?"

"I can try, sir."

"All right, then," decided Strong. "Astro and I will take the jet boats and go looking around. Meantime, you stay aboard and try to pin point the heading on that flash."

"Very well, sir," replied Roger, and turned to the radar to begin the complicated task of rewiring the instrument.

Strong went directly to the jet-boat deck where Astro was busily preparing the jet boats for flight. He looked up when

Strong entered the hatch.

"All ready, sir," he said.

"Very well," said Strong. "I'll take number one, you take number two. We're in section twenty-three of quadrant B. You take section twenty-two and I'll take twenty-four."

"Yes, sir," replied Astro. "Do you think there's any chance of finding Tom?"

"I don't even know if he's out here, Astro. But we can't be sure he isn't. So we'll search and hope for the best."

"Very well, sir."

"Keep your jet-boat audioceiver open all the time and maintain contact with me."

"Why not contact Roger here on the *Polaris*, sir?" asked Astro.

"He's busy trying to find out where the flashing static on the radar is coming from," explained Strong. "We'll make wide circles, starting outside and working in. Blast in a continuous circle inward, like a spiral. If there's anything around here, we'll find it that way."

"Yes, sir," said Astro. "I sure hope Tom is O.K."

"Best answer I can give you. Astro, is to blast off and find out."

The two spacemen climbed into the small craft, and while Strong opened the outer lock, exposing them to the emptiness of space, Astro started the jets in his boat. With a

Carey Rockwell

wave of his hand to Strong, he roared away from the sleek rocket cruiser. Strong followed right on his tail. They circled the *Polaris* twice, establishing their positions, and then roared away from each other to begin their search.

Astro turned his midget space vessel toward the asteroid belt, ahead and below him. Choosing a large asteroid that he estimated to be on the outer edge of section twenty-two, he roared full power toward it. The tiny space bodies that made up the dangerous path around the sun, between Mars and Jupiter, loomed ahead ominously. Moving toward them under full rocket thrust, the Venusian cadet remembered fleetingly stories of survivors of space wrecks, reaching the airless little planetoids, only to die when help failed to arrive. He shuddered at the thought of Tom, a helpless castaway on one of the asteroids, waiting to be saved. Astro clenched his teeth and concentrated on the search, determined to investigate every stone large enough to support an Earthman.

Miles away, no longer visible to Astro and out of sight of the giant rocket cruiser, Captain Strong felt the same helplessness as he approached the asteroid belt from a different angle. He realized any number of things could have happened on the pirate-ship. Tom could have been captured, or if not yet discovered, unable to escape from the ship. Strong's throat choked up with fierce pride over the gallant effort Tom had made to warn the Solar Guard of the *Avenger's* position.

As he neared the outer edges of the belt, he concentrated on guiding his small ship in and around the drifting asteroids, his eyes constantly sweeping the area around him for some sign of a drifting space-suited figure. What Strong really hoped for was the sight of a jet boat, since in a jet boat, Tom would have a better chance of survival.

The young captain reached the outer edge of his search perimeter, turned the small ship into a long-sweeping curve, and flipped on the audioceiver.

"Attention! Attention! Jet boat one to jet boat two! Come in, Astro!"

Across the wide abyss of space that separated the two men, Astro heard his skipper's voice crackle in his headphones.

"Astro here, sir," he replied.

"I'm beginning my sweep, Astro. Any luck?"

"Not a thing, sir."

"All right. Let's go, and keep a sharp eye out."

"Aye, aye, sir," replied Astro. He could not keep the worry out of his voice, and Strong, many miles away, nodded in silent agreement with Astro's feelings.

*   *   *   *   *

The *Avenger* had long since disappeared and Tom was left alone in space in the tiny jet boat. To conserve his oxygen supply, the curly-haired cadet had set the controls of his boat on a steady orbit around one of the larger asteroids and lay down quietly on the deck. One of the first lessons he had learned at Space Academy was, during an emergency in space when oxygen was low, to lie down and breath as slowly as possible. And, if possible, to go to sleep. Sleep, under such conditions, served two purposes. While relaxed in sleep, the body used less oxygen and should help fail to arrive, the victim would slip into a suffocating unconsciousness, not knowing if and when death took the place of life.

Tom lay on the deck of the small vessel and stared at the distant stars through the clear crystal roof of his jet boat. He breathed as lightly as he could, taking short, slight breaths, holding them as long as he could and then exhaling only when his lungs felt as if they would burst. He could see Regulus overhead, and Sirius, the two great stars shining brilliantly in the absolute blackness of space. He raised himself slowly on one elbow and looked at the oxygen indicator. He saw that the needle had dropped past the empty mark. He knew it wouldn't be long now. And he knew what he had to do. He took a last long look at the two giant stars, and then closed his eyes.

Tom no longer tried to control his breathing, but took deep satisfying lungfuls of oxygen and in a few moments slipped into a sound sleep.

The jet boat roared on, carrying its sleeping occupant in an endless spiral around the nameless asteroid.

Not too many miles away, alone on the radar bridge of the giant rocket cruiser, Roger Manning, sweat popping out on his forehead, was trying the radar scanner on the three-hundred-and-tenth point on the compass. He connected the wires, glanced at the scanner, and shook his head disgustedly. The scanner screen was still dark. Having adjusted the delicate mechanism to eliminate the white flashes of static, he couldn't find them again. He sat back in his chair for a moment, mopping his brow and watching the white hairline in its continuous swing around the face of the scope. As the line swept to the top of the screen, he saw the blip outline of a jet boat and recognized it as one belonging to the *Polaris*. Then, slowly, the line swept down and Roger suddenly saw the blip outline of a second craft. With the experienced eye of a radar veteran, Roger was able not only to distinguish the jet boats from the asteroids, but from each other. He gripped the edge of the instrument and shouted at the top of his voice. The second boat was a different model!

He reached for the audioceiver and switched it on.

"Attention! Attention! Captain Strong! Astro! Come in! This is Manning aboard the *Polaris*! Come in!"

Strong and Astro replied almost together.

"Strong here!"

"Astro here!"

"I've spotted a jet boat!" Roger shouted. "You think it might be—"

"Where?" bawled Astro before Roger could finish. "Where is it, you rockethead?"

"As close as I can figure it, he's circling an asteroid, a big one, at the intersection of sections twenty-one and twenty-two!"

"Twenty-one and twenty-two! Got it!" yelled Astro.

"I'll meet you there, Astro!" said Strong.

Astro and Strong turned their small ships in the direction of the intersecting space sections. Astro was the first to spot the asteroid, but for a moment he couldn't see the jet boat on the opposite side of the small celestial body. Meanwhile, Strong, coming from the other direction, saw the boat and relayed the position to Astro. In a few moments the two space craft had regulated their speeds to that of Tom's ship and were hastily donning space suits. A quick look inside had shown them Tom's sleeping body. As Astro started to open the crystal hatch of his ship to cross over to the other, Strong yelled over the audioceiver.

"Astro, wait!"

Astro looked across at the captain's ship questioningly.

"Tom isn't in a space suit. If we open the hatch it would kill him. We've got to tow him back to the *Polaris* and get his boat inside the air lock before we can open the hatch!"

Without a word, Astro nodded, ducked inside his ship, and climbed out again with a length of rope. Working quickly, he tied one end securely to the bow of Tom's jet boat and made the other end fast to the stern of his. Then returning to his cockpit, he sent the jet boat hurtling back toward the *Polaris*.

But he was still faced with the problem of getting Tom's jet boat inside the air lock. It was still under acceleration and there was no way to get inside to stop its jet motors. Astro called to Strong and explained the situation to him.

"Looks like the only thing we can do, sir, is keep going until it runs out of fuel."

"That might take too long, Astro," replied Strong. "No telling how much oxygen Tom has left."

"There's nothing else we can do, sir," replied Astro. "We can't brake her to land inside the *Polaris* and we can't open the hatch to turn off the motor. We'll have to take a chance on Tom lasting until it runs out of fuel!"

Inside the roaring craft, Tom suddenly opened his eyes. He began to cough. There was a roaring in his ears. The stars overhead swam dizzily. And then, as though through a billowing mist, he saw the jet boat ahead of him and the rope tied to his ship. He realized he had been rescued. He tried to signal them. He had to let them know he needed oxygen. He tried to reach the communicator near the control panel but could not lift his arm. He fell back to the deck gasping for air; his lungs screaming for oxygen. Something, thought Tom through the haze that fogged his brain, something to signal them. Then, with the last of his strength, he raised up on one elbow and reached for the acceleration lever. His fingers trembled a few inches away from their goal. His face began to turn violent red. He strained a little more. The lever was an inch away. Finally, with the very last ounce of his strength, he touched the lever and pulled it back by the weight of his falling body.

Even before the black cloud swept over him, Tom could hear the jets become silent. He had signaled them. He had stopped the jet boat. They would know, now, how to save him.

CHAPTER 16

"... and you never picked up that static flash again, eh?" mused Strong, looking at Roger. "Well, the only reason I can think of is that someone aboard the *Avenger* must have discovered what was happening."

"That's the way I figure it, sir," replied Roger.

The Solar Guard captain studied the scanner that was now working in perfect order. "It's a tough break that we couldn't get that fix on Coxine's position. I was counting on it. But at least we found Tom. That's plenty to be thankful for."

"How is he, sir?" asked Roger.

"He'll be all right," replied the Solar Guard captain, his face showing the strain of the past weeks. "We gave him pure oxygen and he came to long enough to tell us what happened aboard the *Avenger*. Get me teleceiver contact with Space Academy as soon as possible. I've got to send a report to Commander Walters."

"Right, sir."

"You've done a good job, Manning. Your work here on the radar bridge did as much toward saving Tom's life as anything."

"Thank you, sir. After what Tom did on the *Avenger*, though, I don't feel like I've done very much. It took real courage to go aboard that ship with Coxine."

Strong smiled wearily. "Well, the boy is safe now and we have a good idea what part of the belt Coxine is operating in. With a little luck and a thorough fleet patrol, we might be able to get him before he can do any more harm."

Strong went below to the cadet's quarters where Astro was sitting quietly, watching Tom. The cadet was sound asleep. When Strong entered, Astro held a finger to his lips and met the captain at the door.

"How is he?" whispered Strong.

"He's been sleeping since he spoke to you, sir," said Astro. "He's pretty weak, but I don't think there's anything seriously wrong with him. After a good rest, he'll be as good as new."

"Thank the universe for that," breathed Strong. He glanced at the sleeping cadet and then turned back to Astro. "Better take your station. He'll be all right now. I want to get back to the Academy as soon as I can."

"Yes, sir."

"Attention, Captain Strong," Roger's voice crackled over the intercom loud-speaker. "I've made contact with Commander Walters at Space Academy, sir. He's standing by for your report."

Strong returned to the control deck where he saw the sharp image of the Space Academy commander waiting on the teleceiver screen.

Carey Rockwell

He told the grim-faced senior officer of discovering the static Morse code flashes sent out by Tom from the Avenger and the race to save Tom's life. When he finished, the commander's face seemed to relax.

"When Corbett wakes up, give him my personal congratulations, Steve. That goes for Astro, Roger, and yourself, as well."

"Thank you, sir," said Strong. "Since Coxine seems to be operating exclusively out of the asteroid belt, I think it would be a good idea to concentrate the entire fleet of patrol ships in that area."

"Good idea! I'll set it up. But get back here as soon as possible, Steve. Coxine and that crew on the *Avenger* aren't sitting still."

"What do you mean, sir?"

"In the last three days we've had reports from seven ships. Jet liners, passenger freighters, and supply ships. All were attacked by the *Avenger* and stripped of everything those criminals could load on their murderous backs. Blasters, paralo-ray guns, whole and synthetic foodstuffs, clothes, money, jewels, equipment. Everything under the stars that they could use. Any ship that even comes close to the asteroid belt between Mars and Jupiter, unless escorted, is a dead space bird. And if we did provide an escort, we wouldn't have enough ships left to carry on the search."

Strong listened to the news with rising anger.

"I'll blast back to the Academy as soon as I can, sir," said Strong.

"Fine!" said the commander. "End transmission!"

"End transmission!"

Strong turned off the teleceiver and called Roger onto the radar bridge.

"Have you got a course back to the Academy, Roger?"

"Yes, sir."

"All right, give it to Astro and let's get moving. Every minute wasted now is the difference between a ship looted and the future safety of the space lanes. I have a feeling that Coxine is not just playing for the hauls he makes on those helpless jet liners."

"I don't get you, sir."

"Look at it this way, Roger," replied Strong with a grim smile. "A man smart enough to do what he did while he was confined to a prison asteroid might have bigger ideas now that he's free. Ideas about himself and the whole Solar Alliance!"

During the weeks following, the activity of Bull Coxine and his pirate crew justified Captain Strong's fears. Repeatedly, ships were attacked on the fringe of the asteroid belt and stripped of armor, food supplies, and valuables. With the secret of the light-key, the vaults of the ships were opened as easily as though there had been no lock at all. The totals had reached staggering amounts and the daring of the *Avenger* was more pronounced, as Coxine struck repeatedly, farther and farther away from the protection of the asteroid belt. It seemed as though he were taunting the Solar Guard with his exploits.

Carey Rockwell

All defense measures seemed to be futile. When the space freighters and jet liners were armed and tried to resist attack, Coxine blasted them into helpless space junk at a frightful cost of life. When the ships were escorted by powerful rocket cruisers, the pirate refused to attack, but the search squadrons were correspondingly depleted. The combinations of the energy locks were changed every day, but with the adjustable light-key, Coxine met every change easily. The entire Solar Alliance was in an uproar, and the citizens of the planets were clamoring for action.

Finally, the commanding officers of the Solar Guard noticed a change in Coxine's operations. Instead of merely attacking spaceships and hijacking their cargoes, he now took over the vessel completely, sending the passengers and crews drifting helplessly in space in jet boats. Three large, fast space freighters of the same class as the *Avenger* were now in the pirates' hands.

Then, one morning, in his headquarters at Space Academy, Captain Strong received an electrifying report. Coxine had attacked a freighter escorted by a Solar Guard rocket scout. Outgunned, the scout had been destroyed, but it had inflicted damage on the *Avenger*. The last report from a dying communications officer on the scout was that the pirate ship was drifting helplessly in space!

Strong, his face showing hope for the first time in weeks, burned the teleceivers, flashing orders to the various elements of the search fleet to converge on the disabled *Avenger*.

"Attention! All ships in quadrants C through M and Q through B-l! Proceed full thrust to quadrant A-2, section fifty-nine. On approaching target you will signal standard surrender message, and if not obeyed, you will open fire!"

Behind him, the three cadets of the *Polaris* unit listened to the decisive words of their commander and then let out an earsplitting yell.

"No time for celebrating," barked Strong. "We haven't caught him yet. He's the slickest thing to hit this system since the reptiles climbed out of the Venusian mud! It's going to be a case of our getting him before he can disappear into the asteroid belt, so let's hit the high, wide, and deep!"

Five minutes later, Strong and the boys were aboard their ship.

"Ready to blast off, sir," reported Tom. The curly-haired cadet's face was still pale and drawn, showing the effects of his ordeal in space.

"Get me direct teleceiver contact with Captain Randolph on the rocket cruiser *Sirius*," ordered Strong.

"Yes, sir," replied Tom. He turned to flip on the teleceiver, and a moment later the captain's face appeared on the screen.

"Randolph here. What's up, Steve?"

"I've got Squadron Nineteen of the Martian reserve fleet heading for the last reported position of the *Avenger* now, Randy. I'll take the point position of your squadron and direct operations. I'll relay course to you as soon as we're in space."

"O.K., Steve," replied Randolph. "I'm ready to raise ship."

"I'll go up first. Form up around me at about five thousand miles. End transmission!"

Carey Rockwell

"End transmission!"

"All right, Tom," ordered Strong, "let's get out of here!"

The young cadet strapped himself into his acceleration chair, then picked up the control panel intercom and began calling out orders crisply.

"Stand by to raise ship! All stations check in!"

"Power deck standing by!" replied Astro from below.

"Radar bridge standing by!" acknowledged Roger over the intercom.

"Energize the cooling pumps!"

The whine of the mighty pumps began to fill the ship almost as quickly as Astro acknowledged the order.

"Feed reactant!" snapped Strong, strapping himself in beside Tom.

A low-muted hiss joined the sound of the whining pumps as Tom opened the valves. "Reactant feeding at D-9 rate, sir," he reported.

"Roger," called Strong into the intercom, "do we have a clear trajectory?"

"Clear as space, skipper!" was Roger's breezy answer.

"All right, Tom," said Strong, "cut in take-off gyros."

The cadet closed the master switch on the control panel and the noise from the power deck below began to build to an unbearable crescendo!

Watching the sweeping second hand of the chronometer, Tom called out, "Blast off minus five—four—three—two—one—*zero*!"

With a mighty roar, all main rockets of the spaceship exploded into life. Shuddering under the sudden surge of power, the ship rose from the ground, accelerated at the rate of seven miles per second, and arrowed into the sky, space-borne!

On the Academy spaceport, ships of Squadron L began to blast off one by one behind the *Polaris* at ten-second intervals. Three rocket cruisers, six destroyers, and twelve rocket scouts. The explosive blast of one hardly rolling away across the surrounding hills before another deafening blast lifted the next space vessel away from Earth.

Aboard the *Polaris*, Roger was busy over the chart table plotting the course when Strong appeared at his side.

"Have that course for you in a minute, sir," said Roger. He turned to the astrogation prism and made careful observations of Regulus, the fixed star always used in astrogation. He jotted several numbers down on a piece of paper, rechecked them against a table of relative values and handed the papers to Strong.

The captain immediately opened the teleceiver and relayed the information to other ships of the squadron. After the *Polaris* had made the course change, the ships followed, taking positions all around the lead vessel.

Like fingers of a giant hand, the Solar Guard squadrons converged on the reported position of the disabled *Avenger*.

From every ship, radar scanners probed the space ahead with invisible electronic fingers for contact with the target. On the *Polaris*, Strong, his nimble brain figuring Coxine's possibilities of escape, hunched over the chart table and worked at plotting alternate courses on which he could send pursuit squadrons on a moment's notice. One thing worried Strong, and that was if Coxine should repair his ship and make the security of the asteroid belt before they could reach him, it would be almost impossible to track him through that tortuous maze of space junk.

Squadron Ten was the first to sight the enemy spaceship, though it was too far away to attack. The commander reported his finding to Strong immediately.

"We still have quite a way to go before we reach him, Strong. But if our luck holds out, we might be able to pin him down in a wide circle."

Strong studied the chart and marked the position of the *Avenger* just reported. He compared the position to that of the other fleet ships and decided that they were still too far away to tighten a ring of armor around the pirate. Strong was well aware that if the Solar Guard could spot Coxine, he in turn could spot them. Luck, mused Strong to himself, was what they needed now. A little luck to keep the pirate from repairing his ship and disappearing into the asteroid belt. He grabbed the intercom and bawled orders.

"Power deck, emergency space speed. Control deck, relay that order to every ship converging on the *Avenger's* position!"

"What's up, sir?" asked Tom from below.

"One of the ships has spotted Coxine. He's apparently still

out of commission, but we're too far away to hail him."

Strong began to pace the deck of the radar bridge, and with each turn, he glanced at the radar scanner where Roger was waiting anxiously for the telltale blip of the *Avenger* to appear.

Suddenly the blond-haired cadet stiffened. He peered at the scanner screen, then cried, "There he is, sir!" His finger pointed to a white outline on the scanner.

Strong took a quick look at the pirate's position and compared it to the positions of the converging fleet. He turned to the televeiver and signaled for the immediate attention of all ships.

"This is Strong aboard the flagship *Polaris*! All ships will proceed according to attack plan seventeen—code nine. Use full power! Emergency thrust!"

As the minutes passed and the Solar Guard fleet plunged forward, the ships forged a solid wall of guns around the drifting pirate vessel. From above, below, and almost every compass point on the plan of the ecliptic, they closed in, deadly blasters aimed, gunners ready to fire.

"We've got him, sir!" breathed Roger. "He can't escape now! Not in a million light years!"

Captain Strong didn't reply. Eyes were glued to the scanner, watching the target and the Solar Guard squadrons, searching for every possible loophole in the trap. Suddenly he spoke into the televeiver.

"Attention all ships! Maintain present range, reduce speed, and take englobement formation!"

In reply, the elements of the fleet smoothly reformed until they formed a giant wheel in space with the pirate ship as the hub. Around and around they flew, all inboard guns trained on the enemy.

As the command ship, the *Polaris* flew high over the formation. Strong checked the formation carefully on the scanner and nodded his satisfaction.

"I think we've done it now, Manning," he sighed. "Coxine doesn't have a chance of breaking through."

Roger looked unhappy. "Ah, it was too easy, sir," he grumbled. "I was counting on having some fun."

"After all these weeks of heartache, I'll skip the fun if you don't mind," said Strong wryly and turned to the intercom. "Tom, check in!"

"Aye, aye, sir!"

"Head for the *Avenger*. Close in!"

"You mean we're going to lead the attack, sir?" Tom shouted in a sudden burst of enthusiasm.

"From the looks of things, I don't believe an attack will be necessary," replied Strong. "We're going alongside to accept Coxine's surrender. Start blasting!"

"Aye, aye, *sir*!"

As Tom's voice was heard over the intercom speaker, issuing orders to Astro for change of course, Strong turned back to Roger.

"Open up the audioceiver to all-wave transmission!"

"You going to talk to Coxine, sir?"

"Yes. And I hope he'll listen. If he doesn't, I'll do my talking with six-inch blasters!"

Roger quickly adjusted the settings on the audioceiver and then turned to his skipper.

"She's all yours, sir. Give it to him good!"

Strong smiled thinly and picked up the microphone.

"Attention, Bull Coxine! Attention, Bull Coxine!" Strong's voice was cold and hard. "This is Captain Strong of the Solar Guard! You're surrounded. You haven't a chance of escape. I demand your unconditional surrender! Acknowledge immediately!"

Strong flipped the key to open the receiver and waited for the reply. Roger moved closer, his eyes glued to the image of the pirate ship looming larger and larger on the scanner.

Fifteen seconds passed. Thirty. There was no sound over the receiver. Sweat began to bead Strong's forehead and he opened the transmitter key again.

"Listen, Coxine! I know you can hear me! I'll only talk to you once more! Surrender or you'll be blasted into protons! I'll give you exactly thirty seconds to make up your mind!"

Again Strong opened the receiver key and waited, but as the seconds ticked by, there was no answer.

"Sir, do you think he's sucking us into a trap?" Roger whispered.

"Maybe," replied Strong grimly. "But he knows what would happen to him if he opened fire."

"Captain Strong! Captain Strong!" Tom's voice suddenly blared over the ship's intercom.

"Don't bother me now, Corbett," replied Strong irritably.

"But, sir," Tom persisted, "that isn't the *Avenger*!"

"What!" Strong was thunderstruck.

"No, sir," continued the young cadet. "I'm looking at her right now on my control-deck scanner. It's the same model ship as the *Avenger*, but it isn't Coxine's!"

"Are you sure?"

"Positive, sir. I was on her long enough to know."

"Blast it! Then what—?"

Roger suddenly interrupted Strong. "Sir, look at her over the magnascope! She's been abandoned!"

The Solar Guard captain quickly turned to the magnascope screen. There he saw a close-up view of the target. It was a helpless derelict. All emergency ports were open and the jet-boat locks were empty.

Strong's face grew pale and he slumped back in his chair.

"What—what do you suppose happened, sir?" asked Roger hesitantly.

"It's easy enough to figure," Strong replied, his voice dull and lifeless. "Coxine is using more than one ship now. And when this one was damaged, he simply transferred to another one. He's outfoxed us again!"

Slowly, with wooden legs, he walked over to the teleceiver.

"Attention all ships! Resume former search stations. All we've caught here is a red herring!"

And as the powerful engines of the *Polaris* picked up speed, Strong imagined he could hear Gargantuan laughter echoing in space around him.

Carey Rockwell

CHAPTER 17

"Spaceman's luck, sir," said Tom, shaking Captain Strong's hand.

Silently the other two cadets in turn gripped their skipper's hand tightly.

"Thanks, boys," said Strong. "If we're going to get that space crawler, we have to trap him. And the best bait I know is a twenty-million-credit pay roll."

"But won't you take at least one man with you, sir?" pleaded Tom. "Sitting up there in space in a decoy ship waiting for Coxine is like—" Tom paused. "Well, you won't have much of a chance, sir, if Coxine opens fire before asking questions."

"That's the risk I've got to take, Tom," said Strong. "It took a lot of talking to get Commander Walters' permission to try this. But we've got to force Coxine to come out far enough from the asteroid belt to catch him before he can run back in and lose himself again." The young captain smiled wanly and added, "Don't think that your job is unimportant!"

Tom, Roger, and Astro nodded. On their return from the unsuccessful attempt to capture Coxine, they had been suddenly faced with the routine duty of transporting a twenty-million-credit pay roll from Atom City to the satellite of Titan for the crystal miners.

Thinking one sure way to catch any rat was to use a lure, Tom suggested that the Titan armored freighter be used as a decoy to capture the pirate, and the cadets could carry the pay roll in the *Polaris*.

Commander Walters had considered the plan, and then realizing that Coxine might fire on the freighter before seizing it, disapproved of placing a full crew aboard the lightly armed ship. Instead, he would send only one man. Strong had volunteered for the assignment and had persuaded the commander to allow him to man the decoy ship.

Now, the two ships, the *Polaris* and the armed freighter stood side by side at the Academy spaceport, and the three cadets and their commanding officer waited for the signal to blast off.

"You have your course for your trip out to Titan, Tom?" asked Strong.

"Yes, sir," replied Tom. "We're to blast off later to-night and take a course through the asteroid belt, traveling on the plane of the ecliptic. As soon as we get through, we are to proceed under full emergency thrust to our destination."

Strong nodded his head, satisfied.

"Do you think Coxine will come out after you, sir?" asked Roger.

"We've tried to make sure that he will, Roger," replied Strong. "It's pretty common knowledge that the Titan pay-roll ship leaves every month, and that it travels a different route each time. Sometimes it goes through the asteroid belt on the plane of the ecliptic and sometimes it goes over. We believe Coxine knows this, and with the thinly guised messages we've sent to Titan, we're hoping he'll try for it."

"But how will you get him, sir?" asked Astro, puzzled. "I mean, with no armor on the freighter to speak of, and no crew aboard, how can you nail him before he gets you?"

"Hyperdrive," replied the captain laconically.

"Hyperdrive?" echoed Tom quizzically.

"I'm going to take the decoy ship through the asteroid belt too, but through a different area, closer to the part we think Coxine is operating in. Seven full squadrons have blasted off ahead of me and taken up positions in that area. When and if Coxine attacks, I'll alert the waiting ships, who'll come in on hyperdrive. By the time Coxine spots them on his radar, they'll be on top of him."

"Then," ventured Tom, "you're staking your life on the ships arriving before Coxine can attack."

"That's right, Tom," said Strong. "If our plan works, we catch Coxine. If it doesn't, at least we know that the Titan pay roll is safe. That's why your job is as important as mine."

They were interrupted by the ground-crew chief who reported the decoy ship ready to blast off.

Strong nodded and the three cadets gripped their captain's hand again. Turning, he climbed into the freighter and five minutes later the Solar Guard officer blasted off from the Academy spaceport while Tom, Roger, and Astro watched from the traffic-control tower.

"Come on," said Tom. "It'll be two hours before we can blast off. We might as well get some sleep. We'll need it."

Reluctantly, Roger and Astro followed their unit-mate from the traffic tower, their eyes full of concern for their skipper. Each was grimly aware that they might never see their skipper alive again.

*   *   *   *   *

"Now shut your traps!" roared Bull Coxine. "The next crawler that opens his mouth gets taken apart!" He stood on top of a table and faced his crew of pirates who were sitting about swilling large cups of rocket juice.

The room in which the giant pirate spaceman had gathered his men was one of many in a building constructed since their arrival from the prison asteroid. Hidden from even the closest inspection by the smaller bodies circling around the main asteroid, Coxine had expanded the small hut used by Wallace and Simms into a huge rambling building containing armories, machine shops, and storage rooms packed with everything he and his murderous crew might need.

Now with a string of successful raids behind them and their personal pocketbooks bulging with stolen credits and valuables, the crew of pirates waited attentively while their cruel but brilliant leader outlined the most daring plan of all.

"Now listen," roared Coxine. "There's a few things I want to say before we start on the plans of the next strike!"

The big spaceman paused and glared at the men in front of him. "Ever since that space-crawling cadet pulled a fast one

190   Carey Rockwell

on me there's been talk about voting for another leader!" He spat the word as if it had left a foul taste in his mouth. "Well, get this. There'll be no voting! I'm the boss of this outfit! Any man who thinks he can take over my job," Coxine's voice dropped to a deadly whisper, "*just let him try!*"

Stony silence greeted the huge spaceman, a silence inspired by fear.

"Now!" roared Coxine, his coarse features changing from a scowl to a broad grin. "The strike!"

This was greeted with a roar of approval. The men demanded action after a week of idleness on the asteroid.

"Wallace!" yelled Coxine.

"Yes, sir," answered the spaceman, stepping up to the table and facing Coxine.

"We'll take up a position in the asteroid belt, here!" He placed a finger on a map of the belt. "Simms!" roared the giant spaceman.

"Yes, sir!" the wizened space pirate stepped forward.

"You remember that rocket scout we blasted? The one that got our other ship?"

"I sure do, sir."

"It's drifting around in orbit near asteroid seventeen. Take a crew of men and a few jet boats and go get her. Bring her back here and fix her up. Strip every pound of excess weight off her. I want a ship that'll fly faster than anything in the system and I want it in twenty-four hours."

"Yes, sir," gulped Simms. "But then what'll I do with her?"

"After you've done what I've already told you to do," snapped Coxine, "I'll tell you more!"

Simms' face turned red, and he nodded curtly.

"Now as for the rest of you crawlers," said Coxine, facing the room full of men. "Repair crews have been assigned for work on the rocket scout and the rest of you will work on the *Avenger* and prepare her for a long flight. I want the three-inch blasters, every paralo-ray gun and rifle, the fuel tanks, food supplies, oxygen circulators, in fact everything checked, rechecked, and *double-checked*!"

Joe Brooks, who had become a favorite of Coxine's, rose and faced the pirate captain. "Where are we going to strike next, skipper?"

Coxine looked at the man with a half-smile playing on his lips. "This operation will have two parts, Joe. The first—well—" his smiled broadened—"the Titan pay-roll ship just blasted off from Space Academy. For the last ten years, the Titan pay-roll ship has been blasting off from Atom City. Now why do you think it would suddenly leave from Space Academy, the home of the Solar Guard?"

The crowd of men murmured their bewilderment.

"I'll tell you why!" bawled Coxine. "Either they have that ship so packed with blasters it would take a fleet to stop it, or it's a trap!"

"But if you think it's a trap," exclaimed Wallace, "you're not going to hit it, are you?"

Carey Rockwell

"I said it *might* be a trap!" snapped Coxine. "But it might not and with twenty million credits to be had for the taking, I'm not going to let her breeze through. I'm going to make sure it's a trap before I try something else!"

"But how?" persisted Wallace.

Coxine looked at his lieutenant coldly. He had indulged the man too long. "I'll tell you when I get good and ready! Now all of you, get out of here and make sure everything, and I *mean everything*, is ready to raise ship at a moment's notice!"

The men got up and shuffled from the room. Coxine turned to his two lieutenants. "All right, Wallace, see that those crawlers do what I told them to do. And you, Simms, get after that rocket scout."

The two spacemen saluted their captain and turned away. Coxine watched them leave the room, already planning his next move, a move calculated to be so surprising that the Solar Guard would be absolutely helpless.

Bull Coxine smiled and turned to study the charts of the asteroid belt.

* * * * *

Alone aboard the armored decoy ship, Captain Strong blasted steadily on his course through the asteroid belt. The young Solar Guard officer was aware that at any moment after reaching the celestial jungle of small planetoids he could be fired on without warning. And though the Solar Guard patrol ships, well hidden in the belt, would blast Coxine out of existence, it would still be too late for him.

Grim-faced, his hands gripping the controls, he rocketed

through space, determined to put an end, once and for all, to the marauding pirate and old enemy, Bull Coxine.

*   *   *   *   *

When night fell over the Academy spaceport, Tom, Roger, and Astro climbed silently into the giant rocket cruiser *Polaris* and raised ship for Titan. Their departure from Earth was routine, with no one but Commander Walters and Captain Strong knowing that stowed in the storage compartment of the spaceship was twenty million credits, the pay roll for the miners of Titan.

Once in space, the rocket ship was put on course and held there by automatic pilot. The three cadets gathered in the messroom and sipped hot tea, staring moodily into their cups. Unable to break audio silence, lest they should betray their position, their first chance of hearing any news lay far ahead of them at Titan. They could only hope that the decoy trap would succeed and that their skipper and friend would return safely. The only comment was Astro's grim prediction.

"If anything happens to Captain Strong," he paused and finished his sentence in a tense whisper, "I'll search the universe until I find Coxine. And when I do, I'll break him in two!"

CHAPTER 18

"Have you got everything straight?" asked Coxine. Simms nodded his head.

"All right, blast off," ordered the pirate. "We'll follow you and keep you spotted on radar. If it's a trap, head for asteroid fourteen, bail out in a jet boat, and let the scout keep going. We'll pick you up later."

Simms nodded again and turned to his old partner, Wallace. "So long, Gus." He smiled. "This is one time the Solar Guard gets it right where it hurts!"

"Yeah," agreed Wallace. "See you later. Take it easy on that asteroid and don't get in trouble with the girls!"

The two men laughed and Simms turned to climb into the waiting rocket scout. The sleek ship had been stripped down until it was hardly more than a power deck and control panel. She was now capable of more than twice her original speed. As the little spaceman disappeared into the air lock, Coxine turned to Wallace.

"We'll give him an hour's head start and then blast off after him. And remember, the first man that breaks audio silence will get blasted!"

All eyes were on the tiny rocket scout as its jets, roaring into life, lifted free of the pirate planetoid. When the speedy little ship had disappeared into space, Coxine turned to his crew and ordered an immediate alert. While the criminals readied the armed privateer for blast-off, Coxine and Wallace climbed directly to the radar bridge.

Joe Brooks was hunched in front of the scanner, staring intently. He looked up when the two pirate officers entered.

"Just following Lieutenant Simms on the radar, skipper," said Brooks. "He's blasting through the asteroid belt faster than I thought he could."

"Lemme see!" growled Coxine. The giant pirate stared at the scanner and his mouth twisted into a grin. He turned away and barked several orders. "Wallace, stand by to blast off in two minutes! Brooks, get me a bearing on that ship."

"You mean Simms?" asked the radarman.

"No! I mean that ship, right there," snapped Coxine. He pointed to a white blip on the scanner. "And after you get the bearing I want a course that'll intersect it in"—Coxine paused and glanced at the astral chronometer—"ten minutes!"

Quickly calculating the bearing and working up the course as ordered, Brooks handed Coxine a slip of paper. The pirate glanced at it briefly.

"What would you say Simms' speed would be if he kept his ship on full thrust, Brooks?" asked Coxine.

Brooks thought a moment. "I'd say it would be about half of what he's making now!"

Carey Rockwell

"Exactly!" roared Coxine. "That's why the ship on your scanner isn't Simms' at all, but another ship!"

The radarman studied the scanner, where, with each sweep of the thin white line, the blip of the ship appeared. "You mean it might be the Titan pay roll?" he breathed hopefully.

"Yeah," breathed Coxine. "I mean it might be the Titan pay roll, and then again it might not!" Coxine turned away, leaving the radarman utterly confused.

Within the two-minute deadline that Coxine had ordered, the members of his crew were locking the last air lock and securing ship for blast-off. Coxine sat in front of the control panel, ready to give the final order that would send the vessel hurtling into space. In a little while, the evil mind, the twisted brain of Bull Coxine would be pitted against the might of the Solar Guard.

*   *   *   *   *

Captain Strong sat on the control deck of the decoy ship, watching the radar scanner and waiting for the appearance of Bull Coxine and his crew. Again and again, the young Solar Guard officer, too restless to remain in one spot, got up and paced the deck.

He flipped on a chart screen and studied the positions of the surrounding asteroids, which he knew hid the Solar Guard fleet, ready to pounce on any attacking ship. Schooled for years in facing the tedium of space travel and patrolling the space lanes, Strong nevertheless was anxious for something to happen, as minute after minute slipped past and no attack came.

Once he thought he saw something move on the scanner and

gripped the sides of the instrument tightly as a blip appeared, disappeared, and then reappeared. Finally Strong was able to distinguish what it was and he turned away in disgust. It had been a maverick asteroid, one which, because of its positive gravity, never became a captive of other bodies in space. It wandered aimlessly through the belt, a danger spacemen feared more than any other, since it could not be depended upon to remain in one position.

Unable to break audio silence and communicate with the hidden Solar Guard fleet around him, lest he give away their positions, Strong found the loneliness driving him into a case of jitters and nerves.

Suddenly he jumped up and stared unbelievingly at the scanner. There in front of him was a blip, traveling at amazing speed, straight for his ship. From its size and shape, Strong could tell it was a rocket scout. He watched it for a moment dumfounded at the speed of the small ship. When he was certain that it was heading for him, he grabbed the audioceiver microphone and began calling hurriedly.

"Attention all ships! This is Captain Strong. Spaceship approaching me, starboard quarter, one-one-five degrees. Estimated speed—" Strong paused and watched the moving blip. "Speed unknown. All ships close in immediately!"

On the scanner, Strong could see the flashes of blips as the squadrons roared out of concealment and closed in on the approaching rocket scout. Over the audioceiver he could hear the squadron commanders snapping orders to their ships as the small ship still headed, unheedingly, for his decoy vessel.

Suddenly the attacking ship slowed and Strong could see the blip turn in a wide-sweeping curve. But it was too late. The Solar Guard ships had it surrounded from every possible angle. The little scout made a desperate dash straight for Strong's ship. In a flash, he saw the plan of the ship's pilot. He was heading for Strong, hoping to use him as a shield from the mighty six-inch blasters trained on him.

Strong grabbed for the control and fired full thrust on his starboard jets, sending the decoy vessel into a screaming dive. The attacking ship tried to follow, but seeing it couldn't make it, turned and tried to escape from the surrounding ships. Instinctively Strong shouted a warning to the pilot to surrender, but even as he spoke, he saw the firing flashes sparkle on the hulls of a dozen fleet vessels as they sent their deadly atomic missiles converging like lightning arrows on the speedy rocket scout.

There was a burst of pure white fire on the scanner and then the young captain gulped as the attacking ship was blasted into a hulk of twisted metal.

Strong grabbed the audioceiver microphone and shouted orders to the fleet squadron leaders.

" ... Squadron L! Put out immediate rescue jet boats and begin salvage operations. All remaining ships will return to Solar Guard base, Space Academy. End transmission!"

Strong hurried to the air lock, hastily put on a space suit, and in a few moments was blasting in a jet boat toward the remains of the attacking scout.

Immediately the communications of the departing fleet were filled with talk of their victory over the pirate band. Strong alone felt uneasy about their success. For Coxine to attack in a light rocket scout, which Strong felt sure had been stripped down to gain more speed, did not follow the pattern which the hardened pirate had established in previous raids.

When he arrived at the wreckage of the rocket scout, Strong found that his fears were justified.

A crew chief from one of the rescue squads approached Strong; his body weightless in space, the man grappled for a handhold on a jutting piece of the twisted wreck, and then spoke to Strong over the helmet spacephones.

"We found only one person aboard, sir," he reported. "And the ship appears to have been stripped of everything but engines and control panel."

Behind the protective glass of his helmet, Strong grimaced. He turned to Captain Randolph. "We've been tricked again, Randy," said Strong bitterly. "We used a decoy and so did Coxine!"

*　*　*　*　*

"They're closing in!" Roger's voice crackled through the intercom from the radar bridge. "Do we fight or do we let those space crawlers take over?"

"Fight!" bellowed Astro from the power deck.

"No! Wait!" cried Tom. "We haven't a chance! If we don't heave to, Coxine'll blast us into space junk!"

Rocketing through the asteroid belt with the Titan pay roll, the three space cadets, under strict orders to maintain communications silence, were unaware that Bull Coxine had outsmarted Captain Strong. Sending in the rocket scout, he had sprung the Solar Guard trap and had cagily scanned the belt for another ship. Finding the *Polaris* easily, the pirate captain was blasting in for the attack.

On the control deck of the Solar Guard cruiser, Tom Corbett desperately tried to think of a plan to outwit Coxine, while his unit-mates urged him to fight back.

"What's the matter, Junior?" Roger called over the intercom sarcastically. "Scared to fight?"

"You know I'm not," snapped Tom in reply.

"By the rings of Saturn," growled Astro, "I never thought you'd surrender to anybody, Tom!"

"Listen, both of you!" shouted Tom. "It's no use! We've got to play this smart!"

"Well, start making with the brains," sneered Roger. "Coxine's in range now."

"Attention—" A harsh unmistakable voice rumbled over the audioceiver. "This is Bull Coxine! Heave to or you'll be blasted!"

"All right, Junior," said Roger bitterly, "company's coming. What now?"

"Cut all power, Astro—fast!" ordered Tom.

"What's the matter?" growled Astro. "Afraid they'll shoot if you don't stop fast enough?"

"Keep your big trap shut and do as I tell you!" snapped Tom.

"Listen, Junior!" snarled Roger. "As far as I'm concerned—"

Tom interrupted him. "*You* listen, you idiot! Don't you see what's happened? Coxine must have found out about the decoy ship, and when we showed up on his scanner, he figured right away that we might have the Titan pay roll."

"So what?" demanded Roger. "That still doesn't let you off for not belting that crawler with our six-inchers!"

"Use your head!" snapped Tom. "With the Solar Guard squadrons on the other side of the belt and with no gun crews on our ship, how far do you think we'd have gotten?"

"You didn't have to surrender, Tom," said Astro. "I could have outrun Coxine in nothing flat. Why, I haven't got half the speed out of this old girl I think she's got."

"A great idea, bird brain! Run away from the very guy the Solar Guard's going crazy trying to find!"

The intercom was suddenly silent as Astro and Roger began to understand Tom's decision and waited for him to elaborate on his idea.

"Now, listen, Roger," said Tom patiently, "we've got about five minutes before those crawlers will be aboard. How long will it take you to make a signal beacon that'll send out a constant automatic SOS?"

"A what?" asked Roger.

"Beacon. One that will transmit on the Solar Guard special frequency and be small enough to hide here on the *Polaris*."

"Why hide it on the *Polaris*?" asked Astro. "Why not try to get it on their ship?" His tone was almost apologetic now that he realized Tom was not planning a cowardly surrender.

"It's a cinch they'll take the *Polaris* over," explained Tom.

"She's fast and she's got six-inch blasters."

"I get it!" yelped Astro. "We plant the beacon on the *Polaris*, and when they take her over, the signal will be going out all the time." Astro paused. "But wait a minute. They'll be sure to search the ship first!"

"First things first, Astro," answered Tom. "Roger, can you make the beacon?"

"Yeah," said Roger, "but it'll take me at least a half hour!"

"You've got to finish it faster than that!" Tom insisted.

"I can't, Tom. I just can't."

"All right, then we'll have to stall as best we can. Get to work. Meantime, Astro and I will find a place to hide it. How big do you think it'll be?"

There was a momentary pause and then Roger replied, "No smaller than six inches. About like a shoe box."

"Could you make it three inches thick, and longer, instead of box-shaped?"

Roger hesitated again. "Yeah, I guess so. Why?"

"Because I just thought of a good place to hide it. They'd have to tear the ship apart to find it, *if* they even hear the signal!"

"Attention! Attention! This is Coxine—" The pirate's voice bawled over the audioceiver again. "You are under my guns. Stand by to receive a boarding party. If you make any attempt to escape, you will be blasted!"

Tom grabbed the microphone to the audioceiver and replied, "Orders understood, but you'll have to wait until we can build up air pressure in the air lock."

"Very well," said Coxine. "We'll give you fifteen minutes."

Tom thought desperately. "You'll have to wait at least a half hour. We broke a valve and have to replace it!"

Coxine's voice became suspicious. "Hey, what're you trying to pull?"

"Honest, Mister Coxine," whined Tom, "we're not doing anything."

"Fifteen minutes," roared Coxine, "or I blast a hole in your ship!"

"Yes, sir!" answered Tom, fully aware that the pirate captain would carry out his threat.

Dropping the audioceiver microphone, the young cadet hurried to the power deck, where Astro waited impatiently.

"Grab a couple of cutting torches, Astro," he said, "and get me a lead-lined suit. I'm going into the reactant chamber."

"What?" demanded Astro.

"You heard me! I'm going to hide that beacon where they'll never find it."

"In the reactant chamber?" asked Astro. "Impossible!"

"Remember when we first arrived at the prison asteroid? How thoroughly we were searched?"

Astro nodded.

"Remember, they even searched the space between the inner and outer hulls? There's three inches of clearance in there. If I cut into that space through the reactant chamber and put the beacon inside, the noise of the jets will keep Coxine from hearing it, and the radioactivity in the chamber will keep them from picking it up on their detectors!"

Astro's face spread into a wide grin, and without another word, he began preparing the cutting torches. Ten minutes later Tom emerged from the chamber and nodded triumphantly. "All set, Astro! Now all we need is the beacon."

Suddenly the *Polaris* was rocked by a heavy explosion.

"They're firing!" yelled Astro.

"Roger! Have you finished the beacon?" demanded Tom over the intercom.

"I need another five minutes!" answered Roger. "I have to set the signal to send out the SOS."

"Will it send out *anything*?" asked Tom.

The *Polaris* rocked again from a second explosion.

"I don't know, Tom," yelled Roger. "I haven't even tested it!"

A third explosion jarred the rocket cruiser and the curly-haired cadet knew that the air lock must have been demolished by now.

"Bring down what you've got, Roger!" he yelled. "We'll just have to take a chance that it'll work. And grab yourself a space suit on the way down. When they blast through the inner portal of the lock, we'll need 'em!"

"Right!" replied Roger. "Be down there in a second."

Astro and Tom hurriedly donned space suits and waited for Roger to bring the beacon. In a moment the blond-haired cadet appeared with the hurriedly contrived beacon. Tom quickly placed it between the two hulls and sealed the hole in the inner hull.

A fourth explosion rocked the ship and the three cadets knew that by now the air lock had been blasted away. They put on their space helmets and climbed the ladder to the upper deck.

Coxine met them near the air lock, two paralo-ray guns clutched in his gloved hands. Behind him, his crew swarmed in and fanned out all over the ship.

But the space pirate stood on the control deck, glaring at Tom. "Whaddya know! The Space Kid himself!"

"That's right, Coxine," said Tom quietly, "only the real name is Corbett."

Suddenly there was a triumphant shout from one of the pirates. "Skipper! The credits! All twenty million! We found 'em!"

Over their spacephones the three cadets could hear the pirates yelling and cheering. Coxine bellowed for silence and the cheering quickly subsided.

Paying no further attention to the three cadets, the pirate captain ordered his men to repair the hole in the air lock and prepare for immediate acceleration. There was a triumphant gleam in his eyes as he announced their destination.

"With the Solar Guard on the other side of the belt, we're going to hit the richest prize in the universe! The colony on Ganymede!"

He then turned and smiled at his three prisoners, adding menacingly, "And we've got three passes to get us through the defenses!"

CHAPTER 19

Ganymede, the largest moon of Jupiter, was an important way station of the Solar Alliance for all spaceships traveling between the outer planets of Saturn, Uranus, Neptune, and Pluto and the inner planets of Mars, Earth, Venus, and Mercury. The colony on Ganymede was more of a supply depot than a permanent settlement, with one large uranium refinery to convert the pitchblende brought in by the prospectors of the asteroids. Refueling ships, replenishing supplies, and having a small tourist trade, it was a quiet colony, one of many spread throughout the system.

With the Solar Guard search squadrons hopelessly out of range on the other side of the asteroid belt, the cadets' only hope of saving the tiny colony lay in the beacon hidden inside the hull of the *Polaris*.

Leaving Wallace and half of his crew aboard the *Polaris*, Bull Coxine had transferred the three cadets to the Avenger and thrown them into the brig. As the ship accelerated toward the colony, Tom stared out of the small, barred viewport while Roger and Astro sprawled glumly on the hard bunks.

Roger finally broke the heavy silence. "What do you suppose Coxine meant when he said he had three passes into Ganymede?"

"Give you one guess, pal," snorted Astro.

"He obviously expects us to give him the recognition signal," said Tom.

Roger sighed. "That's what I figured. But I was hoping I was wrong."

"At least we're all immune to truth drugs," said Astro hopefully. "He won't get the recognition code out of us that way."

"That dirty space crawler wouldn't even bother with drugs," muttered Roger. "They aren't enough fun. He likes to get what he wants the hard way."

"Yes," agreed Tom. "We're in for a rough time, guys."

They all looked at each other, fully aware of what lay in score for them. Finally Astro growled, "I don't care what he does to me. I won't tell him a thing!"

"Same here!" exclaimed Roger.

Tom merely nodded, his face a grim, expressionless mask.

Suddenly three men led by Brooks, the radar operator, appeared in the passageway outside the brig. Brooks stepped forward, opened the door, and gestured with the paralo-ray gun in his hand.

"All right, you punks! Outside!"

Astro started to lunge for the pirate, but Tom grabbed him by the arm. "Take it easy, Astro. That won't get us any place."

"You can say that again," sneered Brooks. "One crazy move like that, kid, and I'll freeze you solid as a cake of ice! Now come on! Move!"

Tom, followed by Astro and Roger, walked slowly out of the brig, and guarded closely by the three pirate crewmen they were taken to the main air lock.

"All right," said Brooks. "The big ox and blondie, get in there!"

One of the crewmen opened the air-lock portal while the other two jabbed Astro and Roger with ray guns. The two cadets stumbled into the chamber and the door was slammed behind them.

"Lock it!" snarled Brooks.

When the men had secured the portal, Brooks turned and pushed Tom roughly along the passageway. A moment later they reached the control deck where Bull Coxine was hunched over his charts.

"Here he is, Captain," said Brooks. "The other two are sealed up in the air lock like sardines!"

Coxine nodded and faced Tom, a thin smile on his face. "I told you I would get the recognition signal, Corbett," he said. "And I will!" Coxine walked over to a large valve on the after bulkhead and tapped the needle indicator right beside it. Satisfied, he turned back to the cadet.

"In two hours," began Coxine, "we'll be within range of the Ganymede garrison and its radar. It takes exactly eight turns on this valve to bleed the air out of the air lock where your two buddies are. So, every fifteen minutes I'm going to ask you for the recognition signal, and every time you say no, I'll turn the valve once. By the time we get close enough to Ganymede to be picked up on their radar, you'll either have given me the signal or your buddies will be dead!"

Tom stood listening to Coxine, his blood boiling at the giant spaceman's cruelty. Suddenly he tore across the control deck and made a dive for Coxine's neck. But the big man met him coming on and with a powerful slap of his hand sent the boy sprawling back across the deck.

"You're a good man, Corbett," said Coxine, standing over the fallen cadet, "but you're a *little* man, and a good big man can lick a good little man any time!"

Brooks and the crewmen laughed loudly as Tom dragged himself to his feet.

"Well, do I get the signal?" demanded Coxine. "Or do your buddies get a little less air?"

Standing unsteadily on his feet, with four paralo-ray guns trained on his body, Tom thought quickly of Roger and Astro, alone in the darkness of the air lock, soon to be clawing their throats for air; of the merciless attack on the prison asteroid; of the helpless ships Coxine had looted. All these things and more flashed through the curly-haired cadet's mind as he weighed his life and the lives of his unit-mates against an attack that would devastate the small satellite of Jupiter. Tom could see through the pirate's demand for the recognition signal. Once inside the Ganymede radar screen, he could attack the Solar Guard garrison and wipe it out before it could raise a ship in defense.

"Well?" demanded Coxine, placing his huge hand on the valve.

Tom knew that if he could stall long enough, the signal aboard the *Polaris* might be picked up by the Solar Guard. Roger and Astro were in good physical condition. They could conserve their energy as soon as they discovered the trap. He had to stall and hope the signal would be picked up in time.

"The only thing I'll ever give you, Coxine," said Tom through clenched teeth, "is a blast of a paralo-ray!"

Coxine snarled in anger and turned the valve, shouting, "One more thing, *Mister Hero*! The minute the air lock is empty, *you* take a swim in space too!"

Tom was prepared for that. He knew the pirate would not take defeat at the hands of a Space Cadet easily. Tom was resigned to his fate. He was ready to accept anything if it would serve the purpose of ridding the solar system of Bull Coxine.

"Tie him to that chair," snarled the giant pirate captain. "And make sure he's secure, or you'll go swimming in space with him!"

Tom was shoved roughly into the copilot's chair in front of the control board and tied down with a thick rope. He winced as the heavy line dug into his arms. After inspecting the job, Coxine dismissed Brooks and the men with a curt nod and returned to his charts.

Tom sat in front of the control panel, his eyes sweeping the gauges and dials and at last fixing on the master acceleration lever. Two feet away was the lever that controlled all the power on the ship. If he could only reach it, he could stop the *Avenger* dead, and possibly even put the ship completely out of commission. But try as he might, he could not get his hands free.

Coxine looked up at the astral chronometer and walked over to the valve. "Well, Corbett," demanded the burly spaceman, "what's the recognition signal?"

Tom only shook his head.

"Must be pretty bad, sitting down there in the dark, hearing the oxygen feed in slower and slower. You sure you won't change your mind?"

Tom looked squarely at Coxine, hatred in his eyes, and he watched the pirate captain shrug his shoulders, turn the valve again, and return to his charts.

The young cadet watched the astral chronometer, seeing the red hand sweep the seconds away, and the black minute hand inch around the dial. Over and over, the curly-haired Space Cadet refused Coxine's demand for the recognition signal and then watched helplessly as the pirate gave the air-lock valve another twist.

Nearly two hours had passed and Tom knew that they would soon be in radar range of the Ganymede garrison. The pressure in the air lock must now be within ten units of zero. Suddenly, overhead, the audioceiver loud-speaker crackled into life.

"Attention! This is Ganymede traffic control. Identify yourself immediately with authorized code!"

Coxine glared at Tom and put his hand on the air-lock valve. "Last time, Corbett. Either you give me the Solar Guard recognition signal, or your buddies are finished!"

Tom gulped. He had no assurance that Coxine would release Roger and Astro, even if he did give him the signal. But he knew there was no choice. He looked up at Coxine.

"Do I have your word as an *Earthman* that nothing will happen to them?" he asked quietly.

Coxine laughed. "Sure. I'll give you my word. I'll even bring them up here so they can see the show and then let you go afterward. But by the time I'm finished with the Ganymede colony the Solar Guard will have your hides for handing out their secrets."

Tom knew what the pirate said was true. He was taking a gamble now. A gamble that by this time his signal on the *Polaris* had been picked up and a fleet of ships would be on their trail.

"Attention! Attention! Identify yourselves immediately!" The voice from the Ganymede traffic-control tower came over the audioceiver again. Coxine's face twisted into a half-smile.

"Well, Corbett, do I get the signal or don't I?"

"Tell them you're a Solar Guard armed freighter." Tom's voice was low. "You're assigned to operation 'Vista.'"

"Vista?" said Coxine excitedly. "Is that the code word? Vista?"

"Yes," said Tom. "Now open the valve!"

Coxine gave the valve a number of turns in the opposite direction and jumped to the teleceiver. He flipped the key open and called Wallace aboard the *Polaris*. "When they ask you for identification, tell them you're working on operation Vista. That's the key word. Vista!"

"Right!" answered Wallace.

Coxine then turned to the audioceiver and spoke in confident, assured tones. "Attention, Ganymede traffic control! This is armed freighter *Samson*, assigned on project Vista. Request clearance for approach and touchdown on Ganymede spaceport!"

"You are properly identified, *Samson*," replied Ganymede. "Proceed on your present course. End transmission."

"End transmission!" roared Coxine triumphantly.

The giant pirate turned back to Tom, bellowing, "Thanks, Corbett. You've just given me the key to everything I ever wanted."

"What do you mean?" asked Tom, suddenly frightened by the strange wild gleam in Coxine's eyes.

"By the time I've finished with Ganymede, I'll have every ship on their spaceport. A fleet big enough to hit any part of the Solar Alliance I want! Solar Guard or no Solar Guard!"

"No! You can't!" gasped Tom.

"Can't I?" snarled Coxine. "I'll show the Solar Guard something they never saw before. Their own ships blasting them right out of space!"

Coxine turned to the intercom, ordered Astro and Roger brought up to the control deck, and then contacted Wallace aboard the *Polaris*.

"Yeah?" answered the spaceman from the control deck of the rocket cruiser.

"We're going in according to plan! Train all your guns on the Solar Guard defense installations and stand by!"

"Ready any time you say the word," replied Wallace.

Jumping back to the intercom, Coxine gave orders to the power deck for full thrust, then ordered the radar bridge to relay the scanner image of Ganymede to the control deck.

As the rocket ship surged ahead under the added thrust, Tom strained against his ropes to watch the scanner and saw the clear image of the colony. He could make out the outline of the uranium plant, the atmosphere booster stations and small buildings clustered around the spaceport. As they drew closer to the tiny colony, Coxine grabbed the intercom and the teleceiver microphones and barked crisp orders to both the Avengers and the *Polaris'* power decks. "Full braking rockets!" roared Coxine.

Tom braced himself against the sudden reverse pressure of the powerful nose rockets, and then, in a moment, felt the *Avenger* come to a dead stop. Watching the scanner again, he saw that they were directly over the Solar Guard garrison. Coxine switched the teleceiver to the colony frequency and spoke sharply and confidently.

"Attention! All citizens of Ganymede colony! This is Bull Coxine. Your entire settlement is under my guns. Any attempt to raise ship and oppose me will be met with instant destruction! Every citizen is hereby ordered to assemble at the municipal spaceport within five minutes. All Solar Guard officers and men will do the same. You have five minutes to comply, or I will open fire!"

Carey Rockwell

The giant spaceman flipped off the teleceiver before anyone on Ganymede could answer. Pressing with all his might, Tom managed to see more of the scanner which suddenly showed the people of Ganymede scurrying out to the spaceport in panic. Coxine watched the activity on the scanner for a second and then grunted his satisfaction.

Suddenly the hatch was thrown open and Astro and Roger were pushed into the room by two crewmen.

Coxine turned to them, smiling thinly. "You owe your lives to your buddy here. One more minute and you would've been walking with the angels. Now," he added to the crewmen, "tie them up so they can see the scanner. I want them to see how easy it is to knock off a Solar Guard garrison!"

"Why you—" Astro lunged toward the pirate but was stopped in his tracks by a blast from a paralo-ray gun behind him. The big cadet stood rigid, motionless, every nerve and muscle in his body paralyzed. Coxine sneered and turned back to the intercom while his men tied up the two cadets.

Tom and Roger looked at each other and, without speaking, knew what the other was thinking. Their only hope was the beacon signal aboard the *Polaris*.

After the men had tied Astro, they released him from the effects of the ray charge and threw him down beside Roger.

"How do you feel?" asked Tom.

"Like I've been run through a set of gears," mumbled Astro. "How about yourself?"

"O.K.," replied Tom. "Was it"—he paused—"was it tough in the air lock?"

Roger smiled. "Not as tough as it must have been on you up here. We realized what was going on as soon as we found out we were losing air."

The blond-haired cadet shook his head and Tom noticed that both Roger and Astro were weak from their ordeal in the chamber.

At the control panel, Coxine was bawling orders to his crew. "Jet boats one, two, three, four, and five! Stand by to blast off!"

The three cadets looked at each other helplessly.

"Russell, check in," continued the burly spaceman.

"Russell here!" replied a voice on the intercom.

"You're in charge of the party. I want you to do one thing, and one thing only! Take the largest ships on the spaceport and blast off. Don't touch anything else! Just the ships. Those you can't get off the ground, leave. We'll blast them later!"

"Aye, aye, sir."

Coxine strode over to the teleceiver. Immediately the image of a man in the uniform of a Solar Guard major appeared on the screen. His voice echoed in the control room.

"Hello, Coxine! This is Major Sommers! Come in, Coxine!"

"Yeah—" replied Coxine. "Whaddya want?" The pirate captain stepped arrogantly in front of the teleceiver's transmitting lens, and from the look on the officer's face, Tom knew he had seen Coxine on his own screen.

"We've followed orders," said the major. "Our only request is that you do not harm any of the citizens—"

Coxine cut him off. "Stow that space gas! I'll do what I please! I'm sending down a crew of men. They have certain orders. Any interference from you and I'll open fire with everything I've got—right in the middle of the spaceport."

Tom gasped. The spaceport was now crowded with the citizens of the tiny colony.

The major nodded gravely. "I understand," he said. "You may rest assured no one will interfere with your men!"

"Huh!" sneered Coxine. "You don't sound so high and mighty now that you're staring into the barrels of a dozen atomic blasters!" He snapped off the teleceiver and roared with laughter.

Tom felt a shiver run down his spine. He could imagine the frustration of the Ganymede garrison, a crack crew of fighting men, forced to surrender without firing a shot. And he had been the cause by giving Coxine the code recognition signal!

Coxine snapped an order into the intercom and a moment later Tom saw the jet boats on the scanner, rocketing down to the surface of the small satellite.

As, one by one, the small ships landed on the spaceport, the three cadets could see the crowds of colonists fan out, allowing the jet boats to come in without interference.

Coxine strode up and down the control deck restlessly, but keeping his eyes on the activity below. Suddenly he rushed to the scanner, stared hard, and then let out a roar of triumph.

The three cadets saw the reason immediately. On the scanner were the unmistakable outlines of two Solar Guard heavy cruisers, four destroyers, and six scouts, hurtling spaceward at tremendous speed. Coxine spun around, balled his fists into tight knots, and shook them at the three cadets.

"I've won! I've won!" He roared with insane laughter and there was a crazed gleam in his eyes. "I've got the ships, the guns, the men, and the secret of the adjustable light-key. By the time I'm finished with the Solar Guard there won't be anything left of those crawlers but what you can hear on a story spool, and the Solar Alliance will be run by one man!" He paused, his face grew hard and he tapped his chest menacingly. "Me!"

CHAPTER 20

"I don't care if the blasted ship blows up!" roared Captain Strong to the power-deck officer of the Solar Guard rocket cruiser *Arcturus*. "I want every ounce of thrust you can get out of this space heap!"

The young Solar Guard captain turned back to the loud-speaker of the audioceiver, turned the volume dial a fraction, and listened. The steady pronounced ping of Roger's signal beacon filled his ears.

When Strong discovered that Coxine had outwitted him, he had gone aboard the rocket cruiser *Arcturus* of Squadron Ten and had continued on search patrol. He dared not break audio silence to warn the cadets aboard the *Polaris*, lest he give away the position of the ship. Later, when the radar officer of the *Arcturus* reported a steady signal over the audioceiver, Strong at first dismissed it as some form of interference from space. But when Titan failed to report the arrival of the *Polaris* on time, Strong investigated the strange sound. Taking a bearing on the signal, he discovered it came from a position dangerously close to the small Jovian colony of Ganymede. After repeated attempts to raise the *Polaris* failed, and no distress signals had been received, Strong feared that Bull Coxine had won again. In a desperate effort to catch the criminal, he took repeated bearings on the signal and ordered full emergency space speed toward the small satellite of Jupiter.

Contacting Commander Walters at Space Academy, Strong related his suspicions and received permission to carry out a plan of action.

"I want you to engage the enemy at all costs!" ordered Walters. "Blast his space-crawling hide into protons! That's an order!"

"Yes, sir!" replied Strong with grim determination. "There's nothing I'd like better."

Six hours later Strong received confirmation of his worst fears. He was handed a message that read:

EMERGENCY:

GANYMEDE GARRISON ATTACKED ZERO THREE HUNDRED HOURS BY TWO SHIPS. ONE VESSEL IDENTIFIED AS ROCKET CRUISER POLARIS. SEND AID IMMEDIATELY. ENTIRE COLONY AT MERCY OF COXINE. SIGNED, SOMMERS, MAJOR, SOLAR GUARD.

Strong realized at once that the cadets had been forced to give the recognition code to the pirate. There wasn't any other way for the pirate to penetrate the defenses of Ganymede. And, thought Strong bitterly, to blast Coxine was to blast the cadets as well. The commander's words echoed again in his ears, "... blast him, Steve! That's an order!"

Strong turned to his second-in-command. "Man all guns! Stand by to attack under plan S! We'll engage the enemy as soon as he's sighted!"

The young officer saluted and turned away quickly. But not before he saw the mist in Steve Strong's eyes.

*   *   *   *   *

Tom, Roger, and Astro watched the incredible scene taking place in front of them with unbelieving eyes. Seven men were standing at rigid attention on the control deck of the *Avenger*. Wallace, Russell, Attardi, Harris, Shelly, Martin, and Brooks. In front of them, standing equally rigid, Bull Coxine was addressing them in a low restrained voice.

"Raise your right hands and repeat after me."

The men raised their hands.

"I hereby pledge my life to Bull Coxine!"

"... I hereby pledge my life to Bull Coxine...." repeated the men in unison.

"To uphold his decisions, obey his orders, and fulfill his purpose of destroying the Solar Alliance and establishing a new governmental order!"

The seven men repeated the words slowly and hesitantly.

"All right," said Coxine. "From this day on, you are my chief lieutenants. You will command the ships of my fleet, and when we destroy the power of the Solar Guard and take over the Alliance, you will help me rule our new order."

The seven men looked at each other, raised a mild cheer, and waited as Coxine shook hands with each of them.

"All right," said Coxine abruptly as he reached the end of the line. "Get to your ships and prepare for full acceleration. We go into action immediately!"

The men filed from the room silently, each with a worried look on his face. Coxine failed to notice their lack of enthusiasm and turned to the three cadets.

"Some day, boys," he said, "you'll go down in history as being the first witnesses to the establishment of the new order."

Astro glared up at the giant spaceman. "We'll be the witnesses to the biggest bust in the universe when the Solar Guard catches up with you!"

"Yeah," drawled Roger in his most casual manner. "You're the one that'll go down in history, Coxine, as the biggest space-gassing idiot that ever blasted off!"

Tom suddenly guffawed. Though close to death, he couldn't help laughing at Roger's remark. The big spaceman flushed angrily and with the flat of his hand slapped the cadet across the face. Then, he turned to the teleceiver and opened the circuit to all the ships that were standing by in space around the *Avenger*, the ships of the Ganymede garrison.

"Stand by for acceleration," he called. "We're going to show the Solar Alliance who's boss, beginning right now! I'll give you the target in a few minutes but head in the direction of Earth!"

He faced the three cadets and sneered. "By the time I'm finished with Luna City, the only thing active will be radioactive!"

Suddenly Gus Wallace could be heard screaming over the

teleceiver, his face a mask of fear and panic.

"Bull! Bull!" he shouted. "The Solar Guard! We just spotted them! Squadrons! Heading straight for us! We've got to get out of here!"

"What?" roared Coxine, turning to his radar scanner. The blips on the screen verified the alarm. He shouted into the teleceiver, "Man your guns! We'll wipe them out right now!"

"But, Bull—" whined Wallace. "They'll blast us out of space!"

Coxine roared into the mike. "The first one of you yellow crawlers that tries to run for it will be blasted by me! Man your guns, I said! This is our big chance! Wipe out the Solar Guard now and the Solar Alliance is ours for the asking! Fight, men! Fight!"

Tom, Roger, and Astro looked at each other, mouths open, not knowing whether they should laugh or not at the dramatic speech of the huge spaceman. But whatever the private feelings of the criminals, Coxine had roused them to fever pitch and the boys could hear them racing through the *Avenger*, preparing to fight the squadrons of Solar Guard ships bearing down on them.

Coxine strapped himself in the pilot's chair and began barking orders to his battle stations, whipping his men into action relentlessly.

And then suddenly Captain Strong's voice, vibrant and firm, came over the audioceiver, demanding the surrender of the pirate captain and his fleet.

"Never!" roared Coxine. "You'll get my surrender from the

barrels of every blaster I have under my command!"

"Then," replied Strong, "I have no alternative but to attack!"

With a coldness that reached across the void of space and gripped their hearts with icy fingers, the three cadets heard their skipper give his squadrons the deadly order!

"Fire!"

Coxine snapped his order at almost the same instant and the three cadets felt the *Avenger* shudder as her turrets began blazing away, returning round for round of the deadly atomic missiles.

Racing from scanner to the control panel and back again, Coxine watched the battle rage around him. With speeds nearing that of light, exhaust trails cut scarlet paths through the black space, as the two opposing fleets attacked, counterattacked, and then regrouped to attack again. The rhythm of the blasters on the *Avenger* had taken on a familiar pattern of five-second intervals between bursts. Gradually, one by one, the pirate ships were hit, demolished or badly damaged, but still they fought on. Coxine, his eyes wild with desperation, now kept lining up ships in his radar sights and firing, with no way of knowing which was friend and which was foe.

Tom, Roger, and Astro watched the dogfight on the scanner in horrified fascination. Never before had they seen such maneuvering, as the giant ships avoided collision sometimes by inches. Once, Tom tore his eyes away from the scanner when he saw a rocket destroyer plow through the escaping swarm of jet boats after one of the pirate ships had been hit.

Fire and change course, fire and change course, again and

again, Coxine performed the miracle of escaping the deadly atomic blasters aboard the Solar Guard ships.

Suddenly the three cadets saw the outline of a rocket cruiser bearing down on them. The white blip on the scanner came closer and closer to the heart of the scanner. Just in time Coxine saw it and shouted for a course change. But even as the *Avenger* swung up and away from the attacking ship, the cadets saw the flash of flame from the cruiser's turrets and a moment later felt the bone-rattling shudder of a near miss.

The control deck suddenly filled with smoke. A flash fire broke out in the control panel and the circuits sparked and flared. Tom was thrown across the room and Roger landed on top of him.

"Up ninety degrees! Full starboard thrust!" roared Coxine into the intercom. "Hurry, you space crawlers! We've got to get out of here!"

Tom quickly realized that in the smoke and confusion Coxine couldn't possibly direct the ship back into the fight. There was only one explanation. He was deserting his fleet and trying to escape.

And then, over the noise and confusion, Tom could hear the sound of struggling bodies and Coxine muttering an oath between his teeth.

"I'll break you in two, you blasted space rat!"

There were more sounds of struggle, and Tom and Roger heard Astro's voice replying grimly:

"Do it and then talk about it, big shot!"

Slowly the smoke cleared from the control deck and Tom and Roger strained their eyes to see through the thick cloud. There, in front of them, stood Astro, torn strands of rope dangling from his arms, in mortal combat with Coxine. The two giants were holding each other's wrists, their feet spread wide, legs braced, grimacing faces an inch apart, struggling to throw each other off balance.

Tom and Roger watched the two huge spacemen brace against each other, muscles straining and faces turning a slow red as they tried to force the other's hands back. Suddenly, with the speed of a cat, Coxine stuck out his leg and kicked Astro's foot from the deck, tripping him. Astro tumbled to the deck. In a flash, the pirate was on top of him, gripping him by the throat. The Venusian grabbed at the hands that were slowly choking the life out of him and pulled at the fingers, his face turning slowly from the angry flush of a moment before to the dark-gray hue of impending death!

Still bound and tied by the heavy rope, the two cadets on the deck were helpless, as Astro's strength slipped from his body.

Tom turned to Roger desperately. "We've got to do something!"

"What? I can't get loose!" The blond-haired cadet struggled against the ropes until the blood ran down his wrists, but it was a hopeless effort.

"Yell!" said Tom desperately. "Yell! Make a noise! Holler like you've never hollered before!"

"Yell?" asked Roger stupidly.

"We've got to distract him!"

Carey Rockwell

Tom began to bellow, and immediately was echoed by Roger. They shouted and screamed. They kicked their feet on the deck and tore against their bonds.

Astro's hands no longer fought the powerful fingers taking his life. There was no strength in the cadet's hands now, but in the split second that Coxine turned to look at Tom and Roger, he gave a mighty heave with the last of his great strength and tore free of the pirate's grasp.

The Venusian jumped up and ran to the farthest corner of the control deck, gasping for breath. Coxine rushed after him, but Astro eluded him and stumbled to the opposite end of the control room, still trying to suck the life-giving breath into his screaming lungs. Slowly his strength returned.

Coxine made another headlong rush for the cadet, but this time Astro did not attempt to get away. He stood squarely to meet the charge and his right fist caught the pirate flush on the chin. Coxine staggered back, eyes wide with surprise. In an instant Astro was on him, pounding his mighty fists into the pirate's stomach and any place he could find an opening. Roaring like a wild animal, the cadet no longer fought for the honor of the Solar Guard or his friends. He didn't look upon the criminal in front of him as Coxine the pirate, but as a man who had nearly taken his life, and he fought with the ferocity of a man who wanted to live.

Again and again, Tom and Roger saw their unit-mate pound straight, powerful, jolting lefts and rights into the pirate's mid-section until they thought he would put his fist completely through the man's body.

Just as Coxine looked as if he would fall, he suddenly charged in again. But his powerful strength restored, Astro stepped back and waited for an opening. Coxine threw a whistling right for Astro's head. The Venusian ducked, shifting his weight slightly, and drove his right squarely into the pirate's face. His eyes suddenly glassy and vacant, Bull Coxine sank to the deck, out cold.

Breathing heavily, the cadet turned, wiped his face, and smiled crookedly at Tom and Roger.

"If I ever have to fight another man like that again," gasped Astro as he loosened the ropes around his unit-mates, "I want to have both fists dipped in lead before I begin!"

He held up his hands. There was not a bit of flesh remaining on his knuckles.

As soon as Tom was free he grabbed the pirate's paralo-ray gun. "We'd better tie this crawler up!" he shouted.

"We'll do that," said Roger. "You try to figure out how we're going to get off this ship!"

Suddenly, behind them, the hatch burst open and Captain Strong rushed into the room, followed by a dozen armed guardsmen.

"Captain Strong!" yelled the three cadets together.

The young captain's face lighted up with a smile. He rushed over to Tom and grabbed him by the hand, then turned to where Roger and Astro were tying up Coxine.

Strong pointed his gun at the fallen pirate. "What happened to him?"

Roger smiled and nodded toward Astro. "Coxine told Astro he reminded him of an ox he saw at a zoo once on Venus.

230   Carey Rockwell

Astro got mad—" Roger shrugged his shoulders. "Poor Coxine, he didn't have a chance!"

Astro blushed and looked up at Strong. "Never mind us, sir," said the big cadet. "How did you get here!"

Strong told them of having picked up the beacon signal. "That was quick thinking, boys," he said. "It was the end of Coxine. If we hadn't stopped him now—" Strong shook his head.

"But how did you get aboard the *Avenger*, sir?" asked Tom.

"This was the only ship that wasn't a Solar Guard fleet vessel, so it was easy to spot. We captured the *Polaris* right off the bat, and after we searched it, figured you three were either dead, or aboard this one. I gave the order not to fire on you, since we wiped out Coxine's fleet before he could do any real damage. When we saw you accelerating, after that last near miss—which incidentally was intended to miss you—we came alongside, forced the air lock open, and took over."

"But didn't the crew offer any resistance?" asked Roger.

"No, and from the story they tell me about Coxine wanting to establish a new order, or something like that, they were glad to surrender. They think he's crazy."

When the enlisted men carried Coxine, still unconscious, off the control deck, the three members of the *Polaris* unit and their skipper watched him leave silently. All of them realized how close the Solar Alliance had come to destruction at the hands of the insane pirate. Finally Strong turned to his crew of cadets.

"Well, boys," he said wearily, "we've recovered the adjustable light-key and captured Coxine. I guess that finishes the space pirates!"

"Yes, sir," said Tom quietly. "And this sure teaches me a lesson."

"What's that?" said Strong.

"Never to think that being a Space Cadet is a matter of learning something from a story spool. Being a Space Cadet is like being—" He stopped. "Like nothing in the universe!"

Carey Rockwell

Choose from Thousands of 1stWorldLibrary Classics By

A. M. Barnard
Ada Leverson
Adolphus William Ward
Aesop
Agatha Christie
Alexander Aaronsohn
Alexander Kielland
Alexandre Dumas
Alfred Gatty
Alfred Ollivant
Alice Duer Miller
Alice Turner Curtis
Alice Dunbar
Allen Chapman
Alleyne Ireland
Ambrose Bierce
Amelia E. Barr
Amory H. Bradford
Andrew Lang
Andrew McFarland Davis
Andy Adams
Angela Brazil
Anna Alice Chapin
Anna Sewell
Annie Besant
Annie Hamilton Donnell
Annie Payson Call
Annie Roe Carr
Annonaymous
Anton Chekhov
Archibald Lee Fletcher
Arnold Bennett
Arthur C. Benson
Arthur Conan Doyle
Arthur M. Winfield
Arthur Ransome
Arthur Schnitzler
Arthur Train
Atticus
B.H. Baden-Powell
B. M. Bower
B. C. Chatterjee
Baroness Emmuska Orczy
Baroness Orczy
Basil King
Bayard Taylor
Ben Macomber
Bertha Muzzy Bower
Bjornstjerne Bjornson

Booth Tarkington
Boyd Cable
Bram Stoker
C. Collodi
C. E. Orr
C. M. Ingleby
Carolyn Wells
Catherine Parr Traill
Charles A. Eastman
Charles Amory Beach
Charles Dickens
Charles Dudley Warner
Charles Farrar Browne
Charles Ives
Charles Kingsley
Charles Klein
Charles Hanson Towne
Charles Lathrop Pack
Charles Romyn Dake
Charles Whibley
Charles Willing Beale
Charlotte M. Braeme
Charlotte M. Yonge
Charlotte Perkins Stetson
Clair W. Hayes
Clarence Day Jr.
Clarence E. Mulford
Clemence Housman
Confucius
Coningsby Dawson
Cornelis DeWitt Wilcox
Cyril Burleigh
D. H. Lawrence
Daniel Defoe
David Garnett
Dinah Craik
Don Carlos Janes
Donald Keyhoe
Dorothy Kilner
Dougan Clark
Douglas Fairbanks
E. Nesbit
E. P. Roe
E. Phillips Oppenheim
E. S. Brooks
Earl Barnes
Edgar Rice Burroughs
Edith Van Dyne
Edith Wharton

Edward Everett Hale
Edward J. O'Biren
Edward S. Ellis
Edwin L. Arnold
Eleanor Atkins
Eleanor Hallowell Abbott
Eliot Gregory
Elizabeth Gaskell
Elizabeth McCracken
Elizabeth Von Arnim
Ellem Key
Emerson Hough
Emilie F. Carlen
Emily Bronte
Emily Dickinson
Enid Bagnold
Enilor Macartney Lane
Erasmus W. Jones
Ernie Howard Pie
Ethel May Dell
Ethel Turner
Ethel Watts Mumford
Eugene Sue
Eugenie Foa
Eugene Wood
Eustace Hale Ball
Evelyn Everett-green
Everard Cotes
F. H. Cheley
F. J. Cross
F. Marion Crawford
Fannie E. Newberry
Federick Austin Ogg
Ferdinand Ossendowski
Fergus Hume
Florence A. Kilpatrick
Fremont B. Deering
Francis Bacon
Francis Darwin
Frances Hodgson Burnett
Frances Parkinson Keyes
Frank Gee Patchin
Frank Harris
Frank Jewett Mather
Frank L. Packard
Frank V. Webster
Frederic Stewart Isham
Frederick Trevor Hill
Frederick Winslow Taylor

Friedrich Kerst
Friedrich Nietzsche
Fyodor Dostoyevsky
G.A. Henty
G.K. Chesterton
Gabrielle E. Jackson
Garrett P. Serviss
Gaston Leroux
George A. Warren
George Ade
Geroge Bernard Shaw
George Cary Eggleston
George Durston
George Ebers
George Eliot
George Gissing
George MacDonald
George Meredith
George Orwell
George Sylvester Viereck
George Tucker
George W. Cable
George Wharton James
Gertrude Atherton
Gordon Casserly
Grace E. King
Grace Gallatin
Grace Greenwood
Grant Allen
Guillermo A. Sherwell
Gulielma Zollinger
Gustav Flaubert
H. A. Cody
H. B. Irving
H.C. Bailey
H. G. Wells
H. H. Munro
H. Irving Hancock
H. R. Naylor
H. Rider Haggard
H. W. C. Davis
Haldeman Julius
Hall Caine
Hamilton Wright Mabie
Hans Christian Andersen
Harold Avery
Harold McGrath
Harriet Beecher Stowe
Harry Castlemon
Harry Coghill
Harry Houidini

Hayden Carruth
Helent Hunt Jackson
Helen Nicolay
Hendrik Conscience
Hendy David Thoreau
Henri Barbusse
Henrik Ibsen
Henry Adams
Henry Ford
Henry Frost
Henry James
Henry Jones Ford
Henry Seton Merriman
Henry W Longfellow
Herbert A. Giles
Herbert Carter
Herbert N. Casson
Herman Hesse
Hildegard G. Frey
Homer
Honore De Balzac
Horace B. Day
Horace Walpole
Horatio Alger Jr.
Howard Pyle
Howard R. Garis
Hugh Lofting
Hugh Walpole
Humphry Ward
Ian Maclaren
Inez Haynes Gillmore
Irving Bacheller
Isabel Cecilia Williams
Isabel Hornibrook
Israel Abrahams
Ivan Turgenev
J.G.Austin
J. Henri Fabre
J. M. Barrie
J. M. Walsh
J. Macdonald Oxley
J. R. Miller
J. S. Fletcher
J. S. Knowles
J. Storer Clouston
J. W. Duffield
Jack London
Jacob Abbott
James Allen
James Andrews
James Baldwin

James Branch Cabell
James DeMille
James Joyce
James Lane Allen
James Lane Allen
James Oliver Curwood
James Oppenheim
James Otis
James R. Driscoll
Jane Abbott
Jane Austen
Jane L. Stewart
Janet Aldridge
Jens Peter Jacobsen
Jerome K. Jerome
Jessie Graham Flower
John Buchan
John Burroughs
John Cournos
John F. Kennedy
John Gay
John Glasworthy
John Habberton
John Joy Bell
John Kendrick Bangs
John Milton
John Philip Sousa
John Taintor Foote
Jonas Lauritz Idemil Lie
Jonathan Swift
Joseph A. Altsheler
Joseph Carey
Joseph Conrad
Joseph E. Badger Jr
Joseph Hergesheimer
Joseph Jacobs
Jules Vernes
Julian Hawthrone
Julie A Lippmann
Justin Huntly McCarthy
Kakuzo Okakura
Karle Wilson Baker
Kate Chopin
Kenneth Grahame
Kenneth McGaffey
Kate Langley Bosher
Kate Langley Bosher
Katherine Cecil Thurston
Katherine Stokes
L. A. Abbot
L. T. Meade

L. Frank Baum
Latta Griswold
Laura Dent Crane
Laura Lee Hope
Laurence Housman
Lawrence Beasley
Leo Tolstoy
Leonid Andreyev
Lewis Carroll
Lewis Sperry Chafer
Lilian Bell
Lloyd Osbourne
Louis Hughes
Louis Joseph Vance
Louis Tracy
Louisa May Alcott
Lucy Fitch Perkins
Lucy Maud Montgomery
Luther Benson
Lydia Miller Middleton
Lyndon Orr
M. Corvus
M. H. Adams
Margaret E. Sangster
Margret Howth
Margaret Vandercook
Margaret W. Hungerford
Margret Penrose
Maria Edgeworth
Maria Thompson Daviess
Mariano Azuela
Marion Polk Angellotti
Mark Overton
Mark Twain
Mary Austin
Mary Catherine Crowley
Mary Cole
Mary Hastings Bradley
Mary Roberts Rinehart
Mary Rowlandson
M. Wollstonecraft Shelley
Maud Lindsay
Max Beerbohm
Myra Kelly
Nathaniel Hawthrone
Nicolo Machiavelli
O. F. Walton
Oscar Wilde

Owen Johnson
P.G. Wodehouse
Paul and Mabel Thorne
Paul G. Tomlinson
Paul Severing
Percy Brebner
Percy Keese Fitzhugh
Peter B. Kyne
Plato
Quincy Allen
R. Derby Holmes
R. L. Stevenson
R. S. Ball
Rabindranath Tagore
Rahul Alvares
Ralph Bonehill
Ralph Henry Barbour
Ralph Victor
Ralph Waldo Emmerson
Rene Descartes
Ray Cummings
Rex Beach
Rex E. Beach
Richard Harding Davis
Richard Jefferies
Richard Le Gallienne
Robert Barr
Robert Frost
Robert Gordon Anderson
Robert L. Drake
Robert Lansing
Robert Lynd
Robert Michael Ballantyne
Robert W. Chambers
Rosa Nouchette Carey
Rudyard Kipling
Saint Augustine
Samuel B. Allison
Samuel Hopkins Adams
Sarah Bernhardt
Sarah C. Hallowell
Selma Lagerlof
Sherwood Anderson
Sigmund Freud
Standish O'Grady
Stanley Weyman
Stella Benson
Stella M. Francis

Stephen Crane
Stewart Edward White
Stijn Streuvels
Swami Abhedananda
Swami Parmananda
T. S. Ackland
T. S. Arthur
The Princess Der Ling
Thomas A. Janvier
Thomas A Kempis
Thomas Anderton
Thomas Bailey Aldrich
Thomas Bulfinch
Thomas De Quincey
Thomas Dixon
Thomas H. Huxley
Thomas Hardy
Thomas More
Thornton W. Burgess
U. S. Grant
Upton Sinclair
Valentine Williams
Various Authors
Vaughan Kester
Victor Appleton
Victor G. Durham
Victoria Cross
Virginia Woolf
Wadsworth Camp
Walter Camp
Walter Scott
Washington Irving
Wilbur Lawton
Wilkie Collins
Willa Cather
Willard F. Baker
William Dean Howells
William le Queux
W. Makepeace Thackeray
William W. Walter
William Shakespeare
Winston Churchill
Yei Theodora Ozaki
Yogi Ramacharaka
Young E. Allison
Zane Grey

Amazon (print on demand) Feb 2010

Lightning Source UK Ltd.
Milton Keynes UK
22 February 2010

150441UK00002B/43/A

9 781421 848013